The Three Essences

The Royal scale of Values

By Marino Lettich

Artist Justin Perry

A rose to the Woman
to the Queen,
because
there is no King
without a Queen!

A redder and more passionate Tea rose to make your wishes come true. T. E. A. : The initials of the essences.

To discover and fully appreciate the first part of the book that deals with "The Three Essences", it is suggested to start reading from the introduction.

Living is an art based on principles and values shared by everyone.

There is no book or secret word that can suddenly transform us into happy beings or allow us to evolve in all fields, however, sometimes even a single sentence read in a book or heard by someone can trigger a change.

First of all, I wish you all a carefree day today as tomorrow.

Here I will share some discoveries I have made in my looong journey, which I consider very important in the search for contentment, well-being and the related evolution that goes along with it.

Many years ago.

All of a sudden, one day I felt as if I had just discovered America: I realized that my thoughts were the cause of my ills, and that avoiding and fighting them was the root of my personal health and growth.

Upon reflection, I realized it is a path all intelligent people take, but it surprised me that the concept was not often recognized as a key factor in the pursuit of well-being: it has to do with psychology, philosophy, the art of living, the research of happiness. To me, the possibility that we can hurt ourselves with our own thoughts was not discussed enough. I felt as if I should have had to inform everyone of the danger. Hence, the beginning of writing a book that should have been named "it pays back", because the cause and effect, the law of attraction that to me meant: "we get, we attract, what we think" or "what we give, we receive" that affects every one of us, opened up my mind.

The subject was interesting, complex; the spark was still burning, so I kept writing. After a few years, my notes became a manual that due to its complexity, I decided to name it "The house keys".

I was convinced that was its definitive name: it touched the key points of the path we need to embark on, to pursue well-being and evolution.

Unfortunately, finding time to write in the middle of all our daily tasks is not easy at all. Although my intentions were always firm, I had a hard time finishing this blessed book. I was unable to complete it; it was like a difficult birth. Only after several years of attempts with many cuts, additions, and undisputed improvements related to my personal growth, something happened: I realized that everything I wrote, referred to three fundamental building blocks that bind together to favor general well-being. I discovered the main essences that categorize and regulate the values of the elements considered most important, to form a Royal Scale of Values that stimulates awareness by simplifying the maintenance of health in the foreground. Focusing on health elevates consciousness: the key factor of well-being and self-realization.

Hence, the last unexpected name change of the book into "The Three Essences", since they were the missing pieces to complete the salient points of the evolutionary path that dictated its rewriting, rebirth, and made it truly original. Only now I am really proud of it, as I am aware that I have accomplished something unique and useful; I do not just mention random elements, but the most relevant ones: the foundations of our awareness and evolution. We all want to feel better, but we also have to merit it. Happiness and health cannot be taken for granted, and the factors on which they depend are innumerable.

We can live in pleasant or terrible places, be rich or poor, lucky or unlucky. Some of us will have an advantage, but our ratings: *the value we give to the essential elements govern our happiness, evolution and health.* Having better views makes the difference; it influences us both mentally and physically. In this process, in which some elements must be overestimated, devalued, or even avoided, eliminated, to feel better and evolve, we must also recognize that it doesn't take much to harm ourselves with our own actions, and that making mistakes and resolving them is the key to inner evolution. Either we learn from lessons, or we will worsen. By contrasting unpleasant thoughts and situations, I understood that something can always be done to improve any sequence of events and circumstances. If I hadn't done anything about my situation, today I would certainly be less happy and in a worse mental and physical state than I am now.

The wake-up call

Realizing that I was the culprit of my ailments.

The first alarm bell rang when I was 24 years old. Due to the stress over the responsibility of managing my first trattoria in Italy, I began having a persistent stomach acidity that would have undoubtedly turned into an ulcer if I had not left the business to go to America. I landed in Nashville as a chef, and after a couple of years I moved to New York, where I opened my first activity in the "Big Apple" and where history repeated itself. Although I was slim and fit (but I must admit, I was always agitated), in just two years, due to the worries about debt, breakup, and a blow I received to one hand (nothing serious, but it was the straw that broke the camel's back), I suffered a heart attack. Is it just a coincidence? Too many variables led me to think that it could have been avoided. Since I remembered that during the heart attack, I first succumbed mentally and then actually fell to the ground, I deepened my research to know if I was the only one who had self-inflicted this condition on himself, or if others like me, without realizing it, had made the same mistake. The conclusion I came to was what I imagined: it happens much too often. This was the beginning of the need to refine the reasoning, improve nutrition, and identify the most advantageous exercises for mind, body and soul, that I will try to share in the best possible way. The first messages I am trying to send are simple: we should be careful, it doesn't take much to get hurt, we do it alone; the negative experience makes us evolve and everything is connected. To express myself in the best possible way, I have divided the book into three parts. The first part covers the value of the essences and their effect on perception. The second part includes several mental exercises to stabilize thoughts and emotions to avoid concerns, mood swings, and ailments. The third one touches nutrition and centers on prevention of physical ailments with a pleasurable self-massage technique that uses a multi-functional tool that I have patented and various household objects, pieces of furniture, walls. All this to: never go down in the dumps, maintain our health, speed up inner evolution, and transform gymnastics into a pleasant self-massage.

First part

A little Philosophy

THE THREE ESSENCES

What is essential for living well?
We can be scientists, physicists, mathematicians and excel in many fields, but be unhappy at the same time, if incapable of keeping our health and mood at the center of our thoughts.
Awakening this awareness, based on the revaluation of some elements, is crucial to evolve.
Giving the exact value to money, relationships, health and intelligence, allows us to administer at best our emotions, mood, and life.
Everything depends on our rating scale: some essential elements need to be valued and others not to be taken into consideration.

The essentialism

Research on Essentialism, which concerns the knowledge of "being" has characterized philosophy from the very beginning. Philosophers from the pre-Socratic era to Aristotle, up to modern times, classify the most important values and principles in the philosophical and physical context as "essential", of greater value.
We need: health, luck, money, freedom, work, company, water, air, sun, food, and to know all the mechanisms that direct our lives and happiness. For all of us health comes first (even though we often do little for it), immediately after we put love and relationships on the list, and then money or luck, intelligence, money. Due to their value relevance, these elements should be considered essences. Of these, health, the most precious, is not always in the foreground (all the daily problems over-shadow it), if we do not change perspective by repositioning the three main essences that govern the scale of existential values.

Paying attention to our thoughts, moods, is the root of happiness and evolution.It is fundamental to identify what is essential and indispensable; only then we properly evaluate and appreciate everything.
Something that describes the essences:

They find a similarity with the primary colors: are indispensable to create the other colors and paint a bright and beautiful picture.
In theology God is the essence – in philosophy it is the necessary part, the most important of a doctrine, concept, principle. To comprehend how our physical body works, and physics, we have to study the D.N.A. and the atom... An essence is: the heart, the nucleus, the central point of the matter.

All connected, never desired enough and indispensable to evolve, without these three undervalued essences we cannot exist and live well.
The first essence should be health, but since one of these essences corresponds to it and is much easier to be kept in mind, *it should take its place to speed up awareness.* This essence is involved in every action and is also always considered unconsciously.
What do we want it to: never end – have so much more?
Sometimes we regret having wasted it.
The less we have of it the more important it becomes.
It is always present in all the daily problems and if lacks, it stresses us.
What we always look at and never appreciate enough?
It is the mother of experience and father of truth.

Take a few minutes before coming to the conclusion.

TIME

TIME

Carpe Diem: take the moment, enjoy the present, make the most of the present time and give less thought to the future because, yes, there is the past and future, but we live in the present.

Time, for its quality and duration, is equivalent to health and humor. Everything has to do with time: focusing on time quality facilitates keeping our mood and health in the foreground.

We work, run to succeed, it's all done "to be on time" or “to gain or save time” and this too often stresses us; it makes us forget that we are not robots. We are full of deadlines: bills, car and house payments, fines... Early or late arrival can cost you your life.

We worry about aging because time is passing too quickly.

Everything is related to time, but we are more concerned with money than time matters. If we lived longer, if we had more time, everything would change. Time has no price, and yet it is always underestimated.

The common saying "Time is money" is a big deception. As we age, it becomes more and more valuable, while the value of money and material assets decreases.

Earning time quality without compromising its length is something that we must earn, it's the prize of smart decision-making.

To focus on time quality, downsize all problems.

We can exploit time better and even gain some of it too, if we search for the essence that controls it universally.

We can't rule universal time, but we have some indirect control over local time, and a crucial one over our individual one, if we keep an eye on the second essence that rules it.

What it is?

Life and longevity depend on this essence that outlines time and there are three types of time:

- Universal, for us it is infinite, not measurable.
- Local, where the rotation of the planets delineates time on earth (in some other places in the universe due to different rotations, gravity…, time, evolution, life, will be disparate).
- Individual, that we can control.

This essence governs time, air, water, gravity, and our thoughts and nutrition are the main forms that direct our time.

What rules time universally? What is it? As long as we have it, we live – the more we have of it, the better it is… Can we name the next essence? Take a few minutes before coming to the conclusion.

ENERGY

Our time available is related to the surrounding and inner energy.
Air, water, food, sun and thoughts are its forms that regulate our life and longevity. We need energy, the more we have it, the better it is.
We absorb and keep it through nutrition, nature, rest and thought.
Energy is involved in any of our actions, so every intelligent person considers the required consumption of time and energy. Searching for it reveals the connection between well-being, intelligence, and the current that guides it. This path expresses time quality through the metaphors of paradise, purgatory and hell, to guide us in the right direction.
From here, a constant "work in progress" should start, to reach the most important goals that improve the present and the future.
Energy is indispensable for general evolution, life depends on it and its amount is connected with the matter. Therefore, our energy and body relate. Synonymous with health and source of intelligence, since fatigue and apathy are opposed to energy, creativity and intuition.
Conserving energy reasonably, by improving lifestyle and regulating our highest sources of its consumption (certain thoughts), makes us earn time. Unfortunately, energy is overshadowed by the importance given to money and material assets, which allows better care and a more comfortable lifestyle. Earning more money is always ideal, but we all get addicted “to have” rather than “to be”.
Basing our happiness on material goods makes happiness volatile, like an income that fluctuates. One cannot be happy with these parameters. Solving this primordial conflict optimizes energy consumption and leads us to discover the third essence, which guides and directs energy, time and happiness. We can have everything, but without this essence, life is not worth living. We can be poor or have physical limitations, but if we have this essence, we are happy.

What is it? What is at the base of happiness? Who is God on earth (for the non-believers too)?
Can we name the third essence?

Take a few minutes before coming to the conclusion.
Since it is an Italian word, the third letter that makes up one of the initials of the rose name on the book cover, you get an extra hint:
it is the most romantic Italian word.

AMORE - LOVE

Without this essence, our time, life, has no meaning.
Our individual energy loses value, and we cannot live well and long. Only if we try loving ourselves and others we: avoid harming people in order not to get hurt in return – take care of nutrition, exercise and thinking – do everything necessary to save energy and therefore save time. Love develops positive energy, enthusiasm, creativity and happiness. Living depends on our own love and can be understood as will power, interiority, desire... but it is always the indispensable guide to achieve any goal. Developed through correct actions, contemplation, meditation, prayers, and practices involving the mind, body and emotions, love is the source of all cures.
It is the predominant element which reveals the communion between philosophy and theology.
At the center of the evolution of our conscience, this positive current, an essential part of intelligence, amplifies itself with positive concepts, views, and the elimination of the negative ones.
Doing everything with love saves us energy.
It allows us to realize anything with less fatigue: it can transform a dull activity into a pleasant one. Without love infants could die, they need to be caressed, embraced, and pampered. The love of our life, the desired person, can be so important for us that living without it can become unbearable, and yet, too often, even when we find what we have long wished for, we do not know how to keep it.
We tend to forget how unhappy we were when we were alone.

To love is to make the desired person and those close to us feel good, and it rewards us by making us feel good in return (the law of attraction, Karma).

Love is undoubtedly the essence of happiness, energy and health.

All religions put it in the foreground.

It is universal and without borders. By avoiding anger, hate, envy, jealousy, greediness, love improves our health, intelligence and happiness; and yet it is not venerated as it deserves.

Desiring the best for ourselves and others, teaches us to know love and ourselves better, to understand that we need more love in our lives, in order to live better.

Love is King on Earth!
It dictates how and how long many
of us will live. Love partly governs
our time: its duration and quality,
Therefore increasing it, gives us some control
over our time and energy.

THE BAD ESSENCE

If there is a divine side, there is also an evil one.

The three essences are positive, and having them, wanting them brings us well-being, but there is one element that contrasts them by stealing our time and energy. What could it be?

It is a well-known element linked to misery and suffering.

It is perceived by each of us differently.

Only with time and maturity do we learn to acknowledge its danger.

It disguises itself with a false appearance that has positive facets not to be discovered. When it approaches, it makes us unhappy and slowly kills us. Every individual is influenced by it, either knowingly or unknowingly.

We must confront this element continuously. It concerns all the daily problems that we try to avoid, but must face if we want to evolve.

To win the battle, we must recognize our enemy.

If something is wrong, we have to look at our points of view, it is insufficient to take a nice walk or a healthy run to release tension. By doing so, you only strengthen your heart and nervous system to endure the damage it causes us. To really fight back, we have to go to its origins. Avoiding facing this evil essence, which unites various forms of aggravations and ailments, causes it to reoccur and puts a brake on our inner evolution.

On the contrary, finding ways and stratagems to contrast it, develops new brain connections (synapses) needed to blossom intelligence and evolution. We have come a long way by passing on even the smallest technical, chemical, and artificial intelligence discoveries.

We cannot state the identical thing about our interiority.
The continuous, sometimes devastating conflicts and crises that we face in a personal and family context prove this failure.
Certain fundamental principles and values are no longer transmitted, and consequently, feelings and moods lose balance, like actions and people themselves. Can we give a name to this evil essence that steals time and energy from us...

Take a couple of minutes before coming to the conclusion.

?

STRESS

Stress exasperates and kills us by depleting our energy, and we don't realize this until it is too late or something serious happens. Eighty percent of all ailments, especially premature ones, are self-inflicted, but we blame money, people, and life in general.
There are difficulties to overcome, but it is our points of view the main culprits for external and internal success and failure.
We are the ones who decide to get angry, hate, be depressed, unhappy or instead to be proactive, happy and open to others.
Analyzing ourselves carefully, we see that there are so many of those aspects to deal with on the inner level, that we should worry about materiality only when we have managed to take in some important values. Most psychological and physical illnesses are caused by stress.
Everyone should just take a look around and ask.
Can it be a coincidence that many, too many people get sick after long periods of stress?
To understand it, we should know the difference between stress and common tension. We study, work and do everything too quickly.

"Let's have it done by robots, as soon as they arrive on the market, I will take two immediately!"
To be able to give, we must have something to share. Being a little tense is therefore normal, while being stressed is an indication of suffering and the presence of limits; a sign of the need for change.

Stress is the "problem of the century"; a dilemma that improves the individual conscience every time we manage to defeat it.

- Stress is the thermometer of happiness: when we lower its level, we are happy, and when it gets higher, we become unhappy.
- To confuse us, it can subtly create energy that seems useful to us, it gives us strength in times of danger and makes us move and work faster.

Knowing it better, however, we can identify its only truly positive aspect:

- It acts as a gauge which tells us what we need to solve.
- It allows us to note the state of the mind-body connection: the physical damage caused by our mind.

Focusing on it raises our consciousness.
Paying attention to what upsets, worries and hurts us,
is as fundamental as focusing our time quality.

THE ROYAL SCALE OF VALUES

The proposed scale with Love, energy and time at its apexes, correct and ideal, in reality it is not so Royal. Knowing how to value its main elements resize all problems, makes us: evolve, happy, lengthens life.

In the conflict between time and money, the latter defeats the value of the essences. Incorrectly and generally, we put materiality in the first place to the disadvantage of everything related to the search of being. "Being" for the effort we make succumbs, and thus being happy becomes more difficult.

Love

Searching love improves our intelligence, happiness, and rewards us with energy. We can recognize it in different forms, which focus on general harmony. Its sub-essences are the virtues: justice, understanding, compassion, forgiveness…

Energy

Energy is derived from positive reasoning guided by love, and nutrition, air, water, the sun, and thought are its sources and sub-essences.

Time

What we can achieve, with the correct use of energy, gives us health and longevity. To earn quality time is a reward; in turn, it allows us to dedicate ourselves to the very important task of the search for love and better well-being.

In addition to these three primary essences, there are sub-essences or just essences. Let's see what they are and how they influence our lives, for better or for worse.

Health

We all agree that health depends on the energy we have, and that a life without physical and emotional health is a difficult life. Although many of us may consider it a primary essence, we have learned that in reality it is achieved by safeguarding the energy and self-love. Health, in fact, coincides with time, because the management of the quality of time automatically puts our health and humor in the foreground.

Intelligence

It is preferable to be moderately intelligent and have health, rather than being extremely intelligent but in a precarious health situation.
Undoubtedly, it all depends on the proportions, but we can study, learn and grow as healthy people, while as sick people it would even be difficult to give ourselves a goal and concentrate on it.

Money

What can we say about this element, considered by many (too many) to be the index of success in life?
We can have it in large quantities, but without health and intelligence, it would be very difficult to be happy, and we certainly would not be able to keep it, work hard and become wealthy.

Luck

Luck is involved in all aspects of life. Being smart and having money could be a matter of luck. Although we have to admit that it is attracted by merit (luck helps the bold), we cannot rely on it, it's a variable that can easily change at any time. We may be born rich, beautiful, intelligent, and with the instinct to be happy, but happiness must be conquered, and in this process, luck cannot be the cardinal point of our action.

WHY ARE THE THREE ESSENCES IMPORTANT?

They are: the extract of what counts the most, the important values - the factors that top any categorization. With them the royal flush of values is created and. Only a proper evaluation of the things that really counts, will balance us. Perception of life depends on valorization.
What is more important than the essentials?

Of:
Taking a nice hot shower when it's cold or a cold one when it's hot; how many of us sing in the shower? - Drinking (a nice beer), when we are thirsty; is it as indispensable as eating (well), and appetite, hunger; don't they make you fully enjoy a good meal? - Being able to wash when your arms hurt - Making love when we get older - Going to the toilet with intestinal problems - Sleeping, when sleep is lacking, being in good company, laughing, being loved, appreciate...
A valuable painting that we will try to sell to a peasant who has nothing to give to eat to his loved ones, will not be sold at any price.

We can be happy, only when we start appreciating the little things. It's easier and more satisfying to do it with what we have (for sure not with what we don't have). It will be difficult to be happy by asking too much and too little, and one can be happy with a little and unhappy with a lot. It's not a question of being poor or rich, but of evaluating appropriately and for sure not to settle.

The essences clarify that:

Love gives energy and buys us time (quality and duration).
Stress: the bad essence, burns energy and makes you ill; avoiding it buys time.

Focusing on time quality and duration, facilitates maintaining health in the foreground.
It awakens and balances us by making us paying more attention to: health, happiness, energetic and depressive thoughts...
We know ourselves, only then do we understand others better.
Only by being aware, we understand and relate to others and time...

The level of emotional intelligence, consciousness, is regulated by love. Intelligence can be divided into several branches and classified as: linguistic, mnemonic, mathematical, artistic... but the emotional one is the most important, it is connected to all branches of intelligence.
Can you outdo yourself if you are depressed?
Is there anything more important than happiness?
The essences clears what is more important and preferable to value.

POINTS OF VIEW

We have all kinds of them.
They involve business, love and relationships,
They influence our perception of life and how we feel.
The points of view we choose to adopt are more important than the reality of things. Some days we will see the glass half empty and in others half full; if we get up in the morning thinking it will be a hard day, it will actually be unpleasant, while if we imagine it easy, it will be a simple one. We decide to feel better or worse without any real change taking place. Unfortunately, too often we just have too few points of view. We could broaden them to solve some situations better. Various factors contribute to form them; the most influential are our family, religion, the place in which we live, circumstances and experiences. Basically stable, at times stagnant and difficult to model, points of view outline who we are.
Forging them requires such perseverance and effort that overcomes any study, in terms of value and difficulty, but it pays off with new and more efficient brain connections that correspond to creativity and intelligence. When you are down in the dumps and want to get better, you analyze the situations and develop new points of view.
Who do we talk to the most? With ourselves!
Sometime, we may even feel that there are at least two "Mees", one intelligent or stupid, one good or bad. To make the right decisions, we must learn to communicate with our intelligent side.

THE COMPASS

How are you? So many bills…
What do we think of, when someone asks us how it is going?

At relationships, health, and all the things that often make us feel worse: bills, taxes, mortgages... In this context, which outlines our future mood and happiness, we should avoid considering our finances because this puts money at the center of our life evaluation.
It is not that money isn't important, but we should remember that it interferes with our well-being.
Putting it in the first position, entering finances as the cornerstone of our evaluations, it makes us go up and down like stock market shares.
We become unstable and unhappy.
Our time quality should not be affected by what later in life we could identify as one of the reasons why we felt too often unhappy.

Some oscillations are inevitable, but the correct evaluation criteria (the orientation of our compass) directs our happiness.

THE TOURNAMENT

If taking life as a game could be a point of view of a long and happy life, it is imperative to train, in order to play well. To play a good game, we should not lose control. Anger, worries and grudges should not prevail, otherwise the game gets ugly, we lose the desire to play or play badly. Never making mistakes will be impossible, but avoiding losing control by staying calm while playing rewards us with serenity, the indispensable ally of victory and happiness. In every tournament, there are many games to be played, and we learn by playing against the strongest. We select our team members: Altruism and Understanding should play in attack, Patience and Calm at the center of the field, Perseverance, Goodwill and Forgiveness in the backfield, while Despondency and Worry should always remain on the field bench with broken legs. What counts is having fun and taking advantage of the difficulties to constantly improve the game. Otherwise, depression, aches and injuries will be common on the agenda. The challenge may not start well, but with the right approach, we will be able to overturn even obvious losses or be rewarded in the finals. Satisfaction, fun and happiness are the most coveted prizes. Each participant in the tournament should consider its starting point, and the tournament as a training in feeling better. We are the first to understand which moves are to be made, and which positions are to take and hold. Every obstacle we cannot overcome will reappear, but we can over-come adversity. Although any type of gymnastics or sports activity is beneficial, we feel good and win games only when we focus on strengthening the weakest points of our body and mind: our views, emotions... some maintenance is required! Who do we talk to most? We sometimes feel that there are at least two of us: one intelligent and one stupid, one good and one bad, so we must learn to communicate with our most intelligent part.

THE GREATEST DECEPTION

It is essential and necessary to have it, but money is always overrated. Taking a point of view that puts it before all the other aspects of our life causes enormous damage to us, and it is almost inevitable not to do at least some of it. We: are always in search of money – go crazy if we run out of money – constantly trade time and money.

Dealing with money teaches us how to evaluate and prize almost everything. There are so many things that revolve around money, so it is inevitable not to think about money.

Although there are many causes of stress, tangible assets are certainly one of the main ones. One of the first words we learn to say is "mine."

The first problems arise in childhood when we are not given the toys we want, or because we don't want to give them to other kids.

In my days, when I was a child in Italy, if we were good, we received all kinds of gifts at Christmas. On the contrary, naughty children, as a joke, got a sugar crisp that looked like coal.

We are constantly committed to comparing everything, to deciding whether what interests us is convenient to have and if the price is right for it. The table is worth $, the painting $$, the car $$$.

Everything has a price tag, and at the right price, we buy it. We are also convinced that money is not that important, but if someone stole our savings or a significant amount from us, or if we caught a thief in our house stealing, we would probably risk killing the thief or getting killed, in order to avoid theft. Before taking any actions, we should ask ourselves how much our life or that of the thief is worth.

Receiving a fine makes us angry, but losing a substantial sum on the stock market could lead us to depression, even if we don't want this to happen. Even when we say we consider money not very important, our emotions prove otherwise.

We should do something to detach from its grip.

If someone asked us what we wanted most or what we put first in our lives, we would respond immediately: health, but we do much more for money.

Nothing is bad about money, if we don't get too dependent on it.

Money is our blood, sweat and tears. For money and success, we often endanger our health, happiness, and lose years of life.

Money is power, and we can do anything for it at the right price.

Someone would even let someone else poop on his or her head at the right price. Fortunately, this service is not in high demand. We also learn to love someone for their money and get married and settle down out of convenience. We undoubtedly need money, and the more we have, the better; but couldn't it be that the greatest effort we make to have it leads us to perceive material goods (even though we may not be materialistic or care much about it) as being more important than our health? Since health is fundamental but not properly evaluated, it is the reason that prevents us from being well-balanced.

Money is needed to cure, extend life, and at the same time it makes us unhappy and sick, since the efforts we make to have it, due to its over-estimation can be enormous and disproportionate.

We need money for the future, for old age, to give it to our loved ones. We, as smart people, have to think about the future, but we may lose our perspective on the present.

Living well in the present, raising awareness, is based on the quality of thinking. We are distracted by material matters, finances, or resolving dilemmas. In the time and money conflict, although time should always win, it usually loses. Money and the search for power have caused more deaths than any virus, earthquake, tsunami…

It is more important than our great-grandchildren.

If we thought more about them, we would proceed differently, but in the end, we are not going to be there, and they are not really so important. The world will most likely end well ahead of schedule, because of the search for power.

Living in the present is what really matters, and money may prevent us from doing it.

Our perception is connected with material values, and that says it all: it is more crucial "to have" than "to be", and that doesn't get along with happiness.
We have more money matters in our head than our happiness.
Will we be able to advise our children, or will they also fall into the materialistic trap we are in? It is not that money is dirty; it is only the means by which we measure material wealth.
It can improve the quality of life and lengthen it. When we have it, we can donate it, and this rewards us by making us feel good.
Unfortunately, money doesn't measure happiness and doesn't guarantee it. Indeed, in many cases it can be fatal, it hides terrible realities: kidnappings, drugs, divorces, falsehoods, personal interests. The real problem is that the more we have, the more we get attached to it; like a drug, it is never enough.
Abundance creates as many ailments as poverty, but we certainly know many people can save themselves because they are wealthy. For all these reasons, when we lose money, we will remember its value, and since it affects health and energy, it should be reevaluated. We shouldn't feel bad when we lose money because we lose time quality, and we may then cry for physical illnesses; the connection is there.

PEOPLE

If we wish, every situation can be understood.

All people who appear "bad" or rude to us are often just angry, ignorant and unhappy. If they learned to act intelligently, they would try to create alliances, not conflicts.

Understanding other people and their points of view is important.

Their negative attitudes could depend on various reasons: they have not solved their problems and are more stressed than we are, they may be going through difficult times and are desperate, they could be sick and we do not know it.

Therefore, given all these possibilities, we should not get angry at them because otherwise we will prove to be equally ignorant.

Sometimes we just can't handle these difficult people: we have so much to do that we forget ourselves, let alone others; however, we must always strive to understand others and why they exasperate us. The way we behave reflects the level of consciousness and related happiness of each one of us.
Perhaps they have understood little from life, and since each of us gives what he or she has, this means they have very little to give; therefore, they are miserable and can be forgiven.

We can't change other people, but we can change ourselves; and then we will see that by correcting ourselves, those close to us will change for the better.

An elderly person may be psychologically underdeveloped, while a young person, on the contrary, may be mature and wise.
If we understand that someone is more mature than someone else and that some may have intellectual or emotional deficiencies, we will manage not to get angry and comprehend all the children around us and especially the child inside us.
If we learned to modulate our expectations, we would raise our levels of patience and tolerance, expand our limits, the ability to understand and intelligence.
When a situation becomes unsustainable, changing the scenario could be the only thing to do, but we shouldn't forget that some negative experiences are useful for understanding our mistakes and raising our conscience.

LIFE AND DEATH

We should not be afraid of dying, but of suffering.
Surely it will be better to die as late as possible, but death should not be viewed as a taboo topic or so negatively. The time may come when it can be desired and serve to live better if perceived differently.
In times of war when life is threatened, some problems which could disturb in time of peace do not subsist. It is enough to eat, to live, to be happy. Expectations drop to essential needs, and we are happy with very little. *The value of essentialism to have a better life is shown here.*
Being aware of the precariousness of life and the possibility of death should improve the present. Imagining, with the right attitude, that we could die tomorrow or in a week, should teach us to live every day as if it were our last, and it's not about going crazy.
Unfortunately, assimilating counts more than knowledge, without it, we can't complete ourselves; knowing doesn't mean perceiving correctly or comprehending! Clearly, given that we are well, most of us will not believe that it can happen so soon and will have a hard time feeling that way. But are we so sure to bet that we won't die before our expectations? We will not bet because we are superstitious and are not obviously sure of what the future holds. We don't know when our time will come, but we are sure it will come sooner or later, so why not appreciate everything more today? How will we feel, twenty years from now?
Or when we are seventy (if we already are, we will look at the ninety-year-old or older, and think that they are very lucky to have reached that age)? Probably worse, if we have not done anything about our well-being. Time passes and must be appreciated; we always have less and less of it available.

THE INTERIOR ROOMS

Avoiding stress is the key that opens the cellar door.

There we keep photographs, old-fashioned clothes, things that are difficult to eliminate, old and useless or in need of repair; an amount of junk scattered around, which prevents us from completing a demanding task: cleanliness and order. Cleaning up the cellar makes us discover other doors, which we could not have seen because of the mess. There are two large doors, and we decide which one to open. One of these leads us to illness, anger, selfishness, unhappiness, while the other to care, understanding and happiness.

The latter is the most beautiful room in the house. We find in it love: *The essence of happiness*. Everything is lovely and precious there, but we will have to learn to appreciate what is inside. It all starts from the cleaning of certain spaces that prevent the raising of values, principles, and essences. In each room there are stairs, which can take us up or down. By deciding to go up, we will make a little effort, but reaching the next level, we will be able to glimpse at the windows from which we can look beyond and from another perspective.

Going downstairs, however, will be effortless, but we will not see or learn anything and go back to the starting point, while going a little up and down, we will experience the usual and common two steps forward and one step backwards, which characterizes each evolutionary path.

The house must however be kept in order. Dirt accumulates and attracts many unwanted animals: negative thoughts, which will become fixed in our mind and no longer want to leave. It depends on us, on the love we have, whether we open one door or the other, and having received little love is not a good excuse for not seeking it; it is always advisable to do so because the path of research is full of gifts. By opening the room of love and ascending, we will understand that appreciating what we have, thanking and having compassion, changes our lives for the better.

Moving from simple appreciation to love transforms everything; only in this way can we raise our good mood and be enthusiastic about life. What would we find if we opened the wrong door?

AILMENTS OF THE BAD ESSENCE

Some recurring thoughts burn more energy than anything else.
The thought causes chemical reactions that create energy or depression.
Depression does not manifest itself without a certain thought.
If something is wrong, we should analyze what to do.
The correct thinking takes into consideration negativity, damages, and ailments. We are not on this earth to suffer, but to learn to feel better and better. Even with the various ailments that will follow one another over the years, by working on ourselves, we can be happier as old people than as young people.
We can change, block or erase negative thoughts, they are the ones who create the feelings and emotions, which are the derivations, the fruit of inner work. Some will turn into depression and then migraines, others into acids and then into stomach ulcers. Those glands like the thyroid will alter hormone production to distort metabolism, damage the heart and liver...
Everything is connected; any physical or mental function can be compromised by these dynamics.
By preventing some thoughts, we can avoid taking pills to feel better or sleep. Thoughts are nothing more than chemicals that we create. The problem is that developing good ones is not that easy, we need time to learn. The care of our mental health requires appropriate enhancement and perseverance.
Going to the pharmacy or to the doctor without considering the internal changes will make the help received by the specialists less effective.
We cannot hope that a tablet alone will put everything in place.
It's up to us to update and rearrange thoughts. Otherwise, we will have to add more pills to our diet.
Prevention is always the best medicine, and it is up to us. If we think that from the moment we get sick to when death comes, it takes time, we will understand that healing will also need time too, and we will not passively wait for someone to cure us. It is all about time!

Thought influences emotions, creates acids, hormones, tensions, that also maneuver the nervous system. The latter is a highway on which energy and information go directly to all parts of the body.
Its mapping allows you to recognize any person.
With his operative center in the skull, the brain, by controlling all the voluntary and involuntary functions of the organism, including the physical, mental and emotional side, is always involved in disease and treatment. Unfortunately, with aging and constant tensions, it loses elasticity and efficiency. One of the easiest symptoms to notice which we all experienced are the stiffening of shoulders and cervical nerves due to persistent mental tensions. In the same way, however, we put tension on the heart, stomach, and other organs that are less easy to feel or notice, but are far more dangerous.
Nervous stiffening will create cramps, which will then favor nerve and muscle tears, which in turn negatively influence all parts of the body implicated, organs included.
After continuous and persistent tension, it will also be normal for the heart to function abnormally. We are almost always born with a healthy heart, but then, with the accumulation of anxiety, anger, and depression, even one of the strongest organs will give up prematurely.
Stress is too often the culprit.
Persistent tension is capable of: altering any physiological process, such as the heartbeat, blood pressure, hormone and white blood cells production – paralyzing the immune system and attract worse ailments such as hypertension, glaucoma, strokes, diabetes, and even paralysis.
When stressed, digestive problems develop.
Who has not experienced acidity after persistent tension?

By creating acids regularly, sooner or later we will generate a small hole in the stomach, which is called an ulcer.
We are subject to anxiety, depression, and when situations worsen, to panic attacks. Depression and stress travel hand in hand, and each one of us reacts differently: there are those who shout and scream and those who get depressed, while others throw themselves or someone else off the balcony. Misfortune is drawn because we are angry or in despair: we fight, drink, and drive imprudently and then have to deal with hospitals and law enforcement.
In extreme cases, drugs are used, physical pain is self-inflicted and suicides or murder occurs. All of this because we didn't face a small problem that grew bigger. When, due to unresolved difficulties, we are restless and sleep deprived, our hearts and brain suffer.
Our throats are under attack when we smoke to calm down because we believe that whoever shouts loudest is always right.
It is useless to ask ourselves why the voice has lowered or disappeared if we add a few more drinks to forget problems.
How many women, when something traumatic happens to them, are subjected to irregular menstrual cycles?
Stress acts on all types of hormones, both male and female. As stress increases, even the most important desires vanish: self-esteem is lost, and love and sexual drive disappear.
How likely is it to affect other parts of the body?
The loss of desire, the inability to have an erection may happen to everyone from time to time; it is almost inevitable and should not be considered a problem; it must be considered normal.
The possible causes are many: a wandering mind, a little nervousness or fatigue, a new relationship, a few drinks.
Monogamy can help stability, but waking up with an erection every now and then (refraining from sex, self-gratification, is advised when it happens), proves that everything works as it should.

Most of the time, we are directly responsible for certain shortcomings. Some thoughts, such as: “it will happen again” (we will not recall our failures, decline, we will visualize the crowning of the act), shut us down. When our thoughts are rearranged, then everything flows in the right direction. We don't have to give too much importance to something that has to happen once in a while (consult a doctor).
Everything passes ; we have to react with serenity, without taking it too emotionally or seriously. Worries hinder reactions, and they often do more harm than the actual problem itself. I had some doubts about how diabetes could be contracted under stress, so I asked an acquaintance of mine, who was affected by it, about how and when the illness started. She replied that she was depressed due to financial issues and her relationship at the time. Not being too sure that stress could affect diseases such as diabetes, I asked another friend of mine who had the same disease the same question, and he too replied that his diabetes came after long financial difficulties.
Coincidences? Too many!
I add another example which involves a couple of my old customers and friends. It happened that, when one of the two fell victim to a stroke that left permanent brain-damage: he was unable to understand and want, the spouse, for the continuous anguish (which I urged to curb) in seeing the suffering of the loved one, subsequently became ill, and shortly afterwards her spleen was removed....
Another coincidence? Because of a sad fact that struck me a lot, since something very similar, but fortunately in a much lighter form, had happened to me, I cannot but mention and dedicate this chapter to the inner beauty, charm, sincerity of a 37-year-old newly acquired friend, owner of a pizzeria.
The last few times I saw this beautiful soul, who had no health problems but smoked a little, he told me that he was rather worried about his business, and that he wanted to change scenery and start over, somewhere else.

Seeing him too tense, stressed, and after hearing his apprehensions,
I remember I advised him to relax, to take it easy and to meditate, because due to stress, I suffered a heart attack. And what happened a few months later?
In the local newspaper, on the front page, I read: "Pizzeria owner dies of a heart attack on Christmas Eve".
In my opinion, this very nice, humble, responsible and caring person, died prematurely from stress-related causes. The problem here is that although I warned him that I had had a heart attack because of stress, and counseled him to exercise and meditate to relax, the whole thing was useless. With this last disgrace that could have been avoided, and after seeing what happened to others for the same reason, to my regret, I must admit that I feel that much of what I have written is of little use. I have noticed that even people who are warned that stress can cause death and disease, find it difficult to counteract it.
Why can't we understand that materiality, worries, anger... can damage our health and even be fatal? Why do we forget our health and that it doesn't take too much to die?
The only reasonable answers to this question are: the attention to one's mental contents is not in the foreground – everyday problems override health in importance (there is a health day of the year, and who knows when it is celebrated?) – it is not given the right value to the most essential elements of life – it is not done enough for our physical and mental health.

Pills of interiority

Fasting cleanses the body: let's do it at least once a month, a year.

Do we meditate, pray, desire, appreciate, relax, and exercise, every day?

Worries are often more harmful than the disease itself.

It is very likely that many present problems in the future will not be considered so important.

Money comes and goes, it shouldn't interfere with our mood.

We can get sick and die or get rich at any time.

Time is never appreciated enough.

Stress resolution is a key to evolution.

If we get angry, we hurt ourselves.

In the face of death, we are all equal, and we must leave everything.

Acceptance brings peace.

Only by understanding our stupidity, we evolve.

Feeling good comes first.

THE HOUSE KEYS

The conscience

Someone knows it better than others, and someone doesn't have it at all. Without this part of intelligence dedicated to the selection of the mental contents that generates energy, we cannot be happy and evolve. Based on: one's own good and also on that of others, the enhancement of time quality and stress resolution, raising the level of one's consciousness increases awareness, intelligence, perception, and the ability to disconnect from unwanted thoughts: it is the key to happiness and evolution!

A low level is connected with hate, despair, anxiety, revenge and depression.

An average level is connected with serenity, inspiration, harmony, forgiveness, understanding and optimism.

A high level is connected with wisdom, happiness, enlightenment, inner energy, and most important of all, with a higher understanding of Love.

Assimilation

It is well-known: that getting angry is bad for your health, but we still get upset – it is not the case to fall in love with someone we do not know very well, or when we perceive something wrong in the relationship, but we fall for it anyway.

In this case and in many others, understanding the error and failing to stop repeating it, demonstrates the lack of coherence between thought and action: a misperception driven by poor awareness, assimilation and evaluation of the essences.

Knowing, understanding, does not mean making a concept, feeling, our own.

Appreciation

Health: the derivation of our inner energy is remembered and appreciated only when it deteriorates rapidly, when we are sick or in the hospital, and then often, as soon as we feel better, all our good intentions vanish.

Too many things to do, too little time, and too many thoughts overshadow our health and mood. Health is often taken for granted, and by doing very little for it, the lack of self-love, the element that avoids unhappiness, is highlighted. We feel the need to be and have as much as possible, to be intelligent and also beautiful, strong, rich and happy. Unfortunately, not everything falls into place, something will always go wrong, especially, while changing plans and goals.

Should we settle for less and be content? Because it is like surrendering, we can remedy it by giving more value to the small things, the essential and most common one, which we more often have the opportunity to appreciate.

If we appreciate something instead of despising it, if we like someone or something, or if we love, if we move from appreciating to loving, everything will change. Only then can we be happier.

Doing something more often for ourselves: appreciating a radiant day, a chat, a massage, a tasty healthy meal, a hot shower... will make a difference, and it doesn't cost much.

Only after appreciating, we can be thankful: a sort of affirmation of luck and contentment. Time will change our perspectives as we age. We will be thankful because: we will see a little better than the day before – a pain in the foot that hindered our movement disappeared – with our aching shoulders, we will be able to shower without others help. These little things will become essential over the years, if we are lucky enough to grow old. Reflecting on the future should make us appreciate what we have now; it will help us understand that there is no need to worry about something that will often turn out to be nonsense in the future. This is how looking to the future improves the present.

Ambition

We should be undeterred and ambitious!
In order to avoid becoming overwhelmed by unhappy thoughts and circumstances, yes, we can be ambitious about financial matters, but we should be particularly ambitious about those issues that affect well-being, health and emotions.
Don't get discouraged, putting time quality in the foreground should be a challenge; there is nothing more important than feeling good.

Desire

The night brings advice, but will it be true? The most fruitful time for good intentions is when we are alone with ourselves, and the one before going to bed is probably one of the best to desire inner changes. We talk more with ourselves than with any other person, it is as if there were two of us to decide: we have a smarter and a foolish part, a better and a worse part, and it all depends on which one prevails.
However, by evaluating all the possibilities, good reasoning attracts the correct behavior. There is a higher consciousness guided by understanding and compassion with which we can communicate at a more elevated level, if we wish ourselves and others well; especially if we include those we do not like much or even hate.
To desire is the most powerful means of internal communication, which doesn't oblige us to believe in some divine power, but only in the omnipresence of Love: the real terrestrial gold or God.
If we desire the best for us, to feel better, to balance material value, to discipline ourselves and change, we will transform ourselves.
That is why the expression "sleep on it" can be useful.

Each of us has a battle to fight, we have to plan our moves to win. Thinking about tomorrow just before going to bed could make it difficult to fall asleep. In this case, our last thing of the day could be to recall everything we have done during the day, from the first step taken to his end, pausing to appreciate the pleasantest moments. It is excellent practice for falling fast asleep, strengthening appreciation and memory. Good night and sweet dreams.

Peace

It is truly the virtue of the strong and intelligent: by slowing down the heartbeat and the physiological and mental processes, it makes us live happier and longer. Let's fill up with it.

Stupidity

Understanding stupidity, especially our own, is a big step towards a better future. Being always smart is almost out of the question; we can be particularly stupid, especially when we have to select the advantageous concepts that reward us with time quality and energy.

Consequently, calling ourselves stupid (not too often) because of our choices and the unhappiness caused by our attachment to material stuff is almost mandatory, in order to understand ourselves better, be happier and keep growing. It is essential to acknowledge our mistakes and that we have many things working against us as well. Only in this way is it possible to face every situation in the best possible way.

Hope

It is impossible not to mention it even briefly, because hope is the last to die. Without it, living is unbearable; hope is an expression of desire, but we cannot live on hope alone if it is not accompanied by action. Having too much of it sometimes can hurt us, but we must not lose it, especially when we are really down.

Hoping that there is something after, that everything goes well, is a step towards the future, but we live in the present, and it is in the present that we catch the moment.

Enthusiasm

We forget to be enthusiastic, to seek a mood that expresses happiness, a condition of excitement and well-being.

One of the most beautiful things to have and look for. Connected with energy saving and our own and others' good, enthusiasm is driven by perseverance, calmness, sincerity and altruism: the allies of intelligence and creativity.

Forgiveness

Although sometimes it would be much more satisfying to settle the score, we cannot live well without forgiveness. Justice with understanding must prevail, but it is crucial to comprehend more to avoid poisoning our blood and mind with toxins of unhappiness. Being unforgiving means maintaining anger and revenge: worms that block our inner evolution and consume energy by making us feel unhappy. A proof of great understanding, forgiveness, and higher consciousness, which certainly benefits the feelings of those who forgive (caring about others resizes one's own suffering), is given by a suffering mother whose son has been murdered, in a country where the law of retaliation, is still in force. This woman, instead of pushing the chair of the man sentenced to death by hanging, she slaps him and forgives him because she didn't want another suffering mother like her. Another proof of the importance of this virtue concerns abandoned orphans.

I noticed the wound healing process can be long and painful, and also that orphans who forgive their birth parents go on and live their lives, while those incapable of doing so, continue to suffer with destructive reasoning. Forgiveness makes us evolve and heals the mind and body.

Thankfulness

Being thankful should be as common as eating, drinking, sleeping and exercising. We could do it before meals, sleeping; whenever it is possible. Expressing gratitude, appreciation makes us feel better; but do we do it enough? Being thankful for: having a healthy baby or having finally found a companion, or for not having a headache or being sick or... But who should we thank? Jesus, Muhammad, Shiva... depending on your faith, and even without believing in God or any other divinity, we should give thanks more often anyway, maybe even just our luck, because many of us, without it, might not be here reading this book (myself at least three times). Thank you for reading the book, and I hope you are enjoying it.

CAPITAL SINS

Why are they called capital? Couldn't it be because they can cause serious ailments?

Envy and jealousy: unhappiness for others' goods. There will always be those who are richer, more beautiful, stronger, luckier than us; for this, we must not be unhappy and rather look at other people's paths to learn. We need virtues, not to desire what doesn't belong to us.

To envy means taking away value from what we have, and consequently, it can only make us unhappy. In the Old Testament, it is called "bone caries"; it means that internal emptiness causes unhappiness. Envy and jealousy are diseases that trigger illogical reasoning, paranoia, depression, hypertension and the blockage of the immune system. Evolution cannot rely on these vices and bad habits.

Wrath: an unstoppable desire to avenge the suffered wrong.

It doesn't matter what causes it, it is always a waste of energy; it stops our creativity and intelligence. Letting it prevail leads to revenge and a series of headaches. Obsessive and irrepressible thoughts push us to take senseless and dangerous actions, we forget our health, diet, exercise and all good intentions. Cultivating anger ruins time quality:

it makes us lose money with lawyers, doctors, it can force us to deal with law enforcement and hospitals.

It leads us to: jail, where we will meet other unstable and sick people, to unhappiness, suffering, and misfortunes. Do we really want to ruin our lives and suffer? Instead, we should try in every way to understand every person or circumstance; otherwise, we will find ourselves with liver, heart, spleen, problems, stomach ulcers, neck tension, and migraines.

Overindulgence and gluttony: exaggerating the pleasures of the table and more. When they prevail, we desire more than necessary and lose contact with our body and essential needs.

By eating more, we create superfluous fat, which makes the pancreas sluggish since the sugar requirement is covered by fat excess. In the long run the pancreas becomes inefficient, and this explains the reason for diabetes, which leads to glaucoma, vascular, gestational complications and renal failure.

Due to being overweight, we are also subjected to sciatica and herniated discs, hip, knee and joint problems in general.

Sloth: indifference, apathy in living and doing good.

A lazy mind has no desires, so we will never reach inner or outer well-being. It will be too laborious to worry about health, exercise, and diet. Due to the lack of movement, circulation, constipation, memory problems will follow.

Aging will be premature, and it will lead to depression and suffering.

Pride and avarice: lust for superiority, lack of respect and unstoppable desire for ephemeral goods. To crave for material goods, to show off, to demonstrate that we feel very good and that we are smarter than others, means that we are fragile and insecure and that we have a long way to go. Keeping everything to ourselves, not considering others, is a confirmation that something is wrong with us. Both vices inhibit logical and altruistic reasoning, prevent a happy life, and this is already a disease.

Lust: uncontrollable desire for pleasure, attachment to earthly goods, vicious and sinful behavior. Lust is too often linked to sexual pleasure without respect. It leads to loss of consideration for others and ourselves; it generates first inner emptiness, and then mental and physical decay; therefore, any ailment will prevail over us.

Despondency: although it is not considered a capital vice, we are very often fed up and tired because of our own fault: we have lost control of thoughts and emotions. We do not consider health, our time quality, and the understanding of the fact that we hurt ourselves.

KARMA – IT PAYS BACK!
CAUSE AND EFFECT – LAW OF ATTRACTION

Everything we do repays us with something similar.
It is a universal law.

Loving someone increases our chances of being loved in return, while if we try to kick someone, let's see what happens after – by seeking love we find it – to study, to learn, expand our intelligence – recommending calmness to others brings us peace – volunteering, forgiveness, decreases our pains.

If we mistreat the earth, we destroy the home of our children, grandchildren and future generations. If we don't care about a neighboring house that is going up in flames, it could happen that the fire will burn down our house or that the unfortunate people, since they don't have anywhere else to go, will come to our house.

People thousands of miles away can affect our lives; it happens constantly that we face immigrants.

How will we stop those who run away from hunger and war?

Can we reject someone in real need?

Anyone who wages war should welcome immigrants!

Even if bombs are thrown thousands of kilometers away, there is always a cause and effect. The repercussion will return by destroying the ozone layer. Consequently, global warming will melt the glaciers, there will be more floods, and the abundance of water will make the little islands disappear.

Bombing pollutes, shatters, the earth's crust, and then we wonder why there are more earthquakes and tsunamis? By shaking somewhere, the energy created will expand and discharge.

What is given is received.

If:

There was only one army, controlled by all
the states of the world.

Those who ordered war went to fight in
the front line.

All the underground resources would belong to all.

Whoever goes to war should have to: pay
the other states for the climatic and natural
damage caused – take the immigrants
the war created.

*There would be more love around, fewer famines,
we could work less, take more vacations,
and be much, much happier.*

EDUCATION

Well-being, understanding and feelings, should be the first subject to study. Wrong parameters prevent us from evolving and having a long and better life. Society, school, could do something more to contribute effectively to the general well-being. School, the basis of individual training, requires a lot of studies but doesn't teach how to study or lay the foundations for improving the emotional state of the individual. Stress resolution, the cardinal point of psychology, philosophy, preservation, emergency treatments, should be learned, studied immediately after learning to read and write.

**We are all unique, but since we are all connected,
we need to evolve together.**

Our unhappiness, madness, frustration, ignorance, badness... affects everyone; we depend on each other.

- When everyone around us laughs or cries, what do we do?
- How would we feel if everyone around us had COVID-19 ?
- How many misfortunes happen because the culprit was unloved?
- When we feel bad, who do we look at, and who takes care of us?

We are a grain of sand in the desert, a drop in the sea, dust in the universe... time passes so quickly, and we go crazy for nothing.

Second part

Exercises for the mind

FOR OUR MIND AND SOUL

Warning.
In the event of serious and persistent malaise, consult a doctor.
With targeted exercises, we will counteract any physical and mental illness. We will not be able to cure leprosy, chickenpox, measles, viruses, but by being fit and strong, we can avoid countless ailments.
Is it not true that the weakest are the first to succumb?
By becoming stronger in all senses: physically, mentally and emotionally, we will alleviate our suffering and heal quickly.
It is important to understand that what consumes the most energy, makes us waste time, years of our life.
Some recurring thoughts devour more energy than any physical activity and sport, and many of these together can lead to devastating illnesses and depression. We need to be alone with ourselves to think and practice targeted exercises that will help us absorb new concepts and consequently save time and health.
Some can be even performed throughout the day, even while working and studying, we can take the necessary actions to stay in shape.
Not doing even basic exercise would be catastrophic. To stop walking could lead to misfortune if some other physical activity didn't take its place. Not using the mind causes an accelerated loss of efficiency that would step up to "deficiency". It is important to work on the mental and emotional side to remember, understand, assimilate, block various thoughts that regulate emotions, moods and health, and we could adopt various practices from different cultures.

THE RECALL

Our mind advances by inserting and removing thoughts and concepts.
Much is based on reenactment, and the best method already implemented by the mind for various purposes can be manipulated and concentrated. When something disturbs us, the stressful thought is repeatedly recalled and associated with several points of view that contrast it. Doing this a few times a day will corrode unwanted thought like a virus. After doing this, we will recall more often the best points of view we came up with to complete the ritual. We will use this method to understand, appreciate and develop a discipline. Inner peace is achieved through meditation, exercise, prayer, good deeds, and, in the most obstinate cases, with penance. It is not necessary to become priests or monks or to climb the Himalayas to meditate and evolve. The problem is that understanding a concept and making it our own is a very difficult thing to do. We can understand many things, but to perceive as we would like, a lifetime is needed to learn. Absorbing and deleting a concept requires perseverance and dedication. If the elaborated concept is not recalled often, it will not be acquired. When we are sick, we take medicine and do physiotherapy exercises even several times a day.

It is basic to fixate in mind what's really important!

BROKEN RECORD

Yes, it is important to insert and delete some thoughts from our mind, but it is equally relevant to disconnect from everything.
It often occurs that we fixate over the loss of money, lack of love?
This can be very dangerous! It is therefore very important to change and stop the coming and going of wild thoughts. In this case, the mind turns and turns like a broken record that, in the long run, will make us feel bad, exasperated, lose control with senseless actions which we could regret.

Using the previous exercise may be difficult to put into practice, due to the lack of acceptance of some views; however, we can get around the obstacle by closing our eyes and listening to the noise we make with our throats or mouths as we breathe out. It will not be easy to detach ourselves from the unwanted, but by insisting on avoiding any beautiful or ugly thoughts, perseverance will reward us. The exercise is to be repeated several times, and varying the noise and its cadence will help maintain concentration.

We will not be demoralized if sometimes thinking takes over.

Just attempting to stop thinking: develops the ability to block the assaults of unwanted thoughts, even when they assail us the next day.

It recharges and allows us to reason meaningfully.

Only a free mind can be happy and creative.

Since thoughts are chemicals created by us, we can develop, reject and eliminate them.

MANY POSITIONS TO DETACH

In any position and even in bed, we could do some of these things at the same time, to detach from all the headaches accumulated.

We could: expel the air through the mouth slowly, hold our breath, keep our chest expanded, join the thumb and forefinger, mentally repeat the words: nothing or maybe yes while inhaling and maybe not while exhaling.

Keeping our mind always busy with multiple thoughts that refer to the same subject to avoid unwanted thinking is another way that can help us to "detach" and find peace in difficult times.

TRICKS TO REMEMBER

It is difficult to remember what is really important when we have thousands of tasks to do and too many thoughts in our mind. We may have to devise some tricks to recall a thought or a concept more often. Here are a few very practical methods to obtain excellent results.

We could: dedicate each sip of tea or soup or a yoga position to a concept – keep a coin in our hands, in a shoe, or put a small piece of ginger in our mouths – put the wristwatch on the other hand or a ring on another finger.

The movements of the things or their unusual position will bring the connected concept back to our mind… And we can invent.

MUDRA

These are superstitious, propitiatory and even aggressive or vulgar hand movements accompanied also by dances, which complement meditations and practices and of various religions aiming to obtain benefits on the physical and energetic field. Holding our hands or fingers in a certain way for the purpose of fixing or removing something from our mind is an excellent method for recalling and maintaining multiple concepts. It can be implemented in any place and combined with any exercise, meditation or yoga position. With this method a single finger can bring to mind a habit, a vice to be controlled, the limitations of a person, the need to do some breathing exercises, to thank, appreciate, desire… more often; and since there are ten fingers, we understand how many possibilities are offered.

MANTRA

Of Indian origin and practiced by Buddhists, Hindus, and others who believe they have psychological, spiritual and sacred powers capable of directing towards enlightenment. This ancient method may involve the practical use of familiar or unique sounds, a distinct syllable, inspired red songs, invocations, and even a group of words chosen individually without a syntactic structure or specific meaning.
A large part of learning is based on repetition.
Assimilating an unknown language relies on repeating the same word inserted in a known phrase as a new road route by retracing it often.
We therefore could utilize the same method to bring a desired concept to mind. We can then mentally repeat a word and combine it with a concept that helps solve a problem.
Some example of words and concepts:

For example:

- "Limits", to understand the incapacity of a person, will avoid
- stress and unpleasant situations.
- "Time", to bring up to us that its quality is invaluable and that we have to learn to elevate it.
- "Good intentions", the creative control of some vice.
- "Game", that life must be taken as a game to live better.
- "Ten", the psychological age or low level of someone understanding, we need to cope with.
- "Challenge", to strongly confront our weak points.

To complete the practice, we will visualize the desired action and behavior.

It is an excellent method to set our mind not to go down in the dumps and to re-evaluate principles and values. All to reduce worries and the importance of the smallest fears that arise from day to day. It is up to us to continue the list of priorities for our well-being.

The most suitable words are those "of the moment", because every situation, circumstance, needs the right word to be addressed in the best way. We can utilize any word we prefer and add other words to the composition and sing them, to convert some Mantra into songs and discover that we may even have a musical talent; Gospel music is an example... If you become rich, do not forget me (.'ᴗ'.).

SOMETHING STRONG

Consult a: psychologist, psychiatrist, doctor, neurologist before reading. The proposed meditation could be precarious for fearful, depressed, and mentally ill people.

Words have a certain power: they can hurt and kill. Many people have died for just one more word, or an unspoken one. Each word vibrates in the mind with its meaning, but some of them are more powerful than others. We will feel better by: reducing stress, the points of maximum energy consumption – focusing on time quality and also on its end. Even if this last thought is undoubtedly heavy in meaning, we cannot but admit that whoever has come too close to death, wakes up, radically transforms itself, and remains no longer the same. In all the near-death experiences, people change, perceive life differently and become less material. Realizing the precariousness of life reduces superficiality: the essential becomes more important – awareness and conscience are raised, and moral values are re-balanced.

To experience life better, the Tibetan Buddhist monks have a notable saying: "every day passed without contemplating death is a wasted day" and then they point out that by being depressed, it is more practical to meditate on rebirth. We will look upon it every day with the right attitude, and we will do likewise with appreciation of the quality of time, our limitations or stupidity, forgiveness...

OXYGENATION

Breathing comes before everything.
Without food, we can live for weeks, without water for a few days and without air only for a few minutes; no physiological activity can exist without it. Oxygen is the best source of energy. Even in moments of maximum mental confusion or laziness, one should never do without at least one breathing exercise because:

- ❖ The most common and substantial benefit of all sports and gymnastic activities is oxygenation.
- ❖ Every living thing, every cell, needs oxygen to start the combustion process necessary for energy production.
- ❖ Where the air is clean, we live longer. Pollution reduces lung capacity and consequently the brain and most important glands, due to poor oxygenation, nutrition, decrease in volume.
- ❖ Under strong pressure, or while running long distances or lifting heavy weights, we gasp for air and immediately after for water, which coincidentally contains one-third of oxygen.
- ❖ When we are really sick and lacking air, lying down with our legs raised increases blood supplies, oxygenation, to the upper part of the body, the most important one.
- ❖ Healthy parts of the body are well-oxygenated, while the unhealthy ones are not.

From all this, we can deduce that to slow down aging and maintain well-being, for the advantage in the effort/reward ratio, breathing exercises are fundamental.
Usually, little is done individually to be well-oxygenated, and even less collectively to keep air clean.

Air is the first element we savor, and the last one we desire.

Here some important exercises:

DEEP BREATHING

Attention: if you already have had heart or lung problems, or take medications, consult a doctor. The exercise is very simple, it is just a matter of: inhaling and expanding or exhaling and retracting the chest and the abdomen as much as possible – keeping it expanded or retracted for a few seconds. We will do it without forcing too much, and intersperse it with regular breathing.

It is a method of Indian origins that should be practiced more often because it allows us to oxygenate the whole body and relax.

Its benefits are: the increased elasticity of the respiratory system facilitates expelling phlegm and toxins. All the muscle groups involved in digestion and evacuation strengthen. Veins, arteries and internal organ flexibility is improved. The heart beat slows down since breathing is in direct symbiosis with thinking. Breathing exercises are to be considered meditation because they affect the body and mind.

Never forget to breathe!

CONTINUOUS MEDITATION

This exercise is of very practical use because: the only thing we have to do is to exhale with the mouth ajar, as if we were inflating a balloon. We can do it anytime and anywhere: comfortably in bed, while walking, reading, in any yoga position... It is a great meditation if we add to it a thought that counteracts stress as we confront its causes.

In terms of energy saved, it is certainly a very rewarding practice: it slows the heart rate, calms the mind and unconsciously puts health (the mood, quality of time) in the foreground.

THE VALSALVA MANEUVER

The Valsalva maneuver is an ancient and simple breathing technique that is used for various purposes. Its first use in the medical field was to expel secretions from the ear in the case of otitis or other infection, while recently it is used to restore and evaluate heart rhythm in the presence of tachycardia.

Something very similar to what we unconsciously do on an airplane or underwater to compensate for the pressure variation. The maneuver by increasing the pressure in the upper part of the body, especially in the head, stimulates the correct functioning of the heart and the Vagus nerve. The most important nerve in the body that keeps the brain, heart, lungs, liver, kidneys, stomach, colon, connected. A sort of control unit that is activated in situations of relaxation and constitutes a large part of the parasympathetic nervous system involved in various tasks: metabolism, regulation of the heart rate, digestion, sweating, speech...

To carry out this maneuver that affects the whole body, one exhales forcefully through the mouth ajar while keeping the nose tightly closed. It can be repeated several times without forcing too hard, and we should wait a bit before trying it again.

PERSONAL EXPERIENCE

I smoked, I drank, I often stayed up in the wee hours, I was a bit of a rascal. So I think that I may have deserved the migraine (it could be also genetic), which made me also discover that breathing deeply and compressing the breath, shortens its course (at the first symptoms I also immediately take an aspirin (consult a doctor for the medicines to be taken). You breathe intensely until you notice improvements.

Third part

If you want something done right do it yourself

THE AUTO MASSAGE

The most important task we have in our lives is to do everything possible to feel better and live longer. To follow this principle, we will consider our diet, humor, exercise, pains, degenerative changes, and even anomalies that appear out of nowhere. By doing so, we will discover that what is done for ourselves determines, more than anything, our well-being. Many ailments can be avoided or treated more effectively by counter-attacking them from several fronts: consulting a specialist, a diet, targeted gymnastics that combine physical and mental exercises to reduce stress and physical tension. The latter, among many solutions, is as essential as nutrition, natural remedies and taking medicine.

The beauty of it is that we can do the most effective and satisfying exercises at home, and without the need for great physical strength. The suggested exercises are suitable for the young and old and oriented towards prevention. They probably transform themselves in the best form of a targeted physical care practice: auto-massage. This is one of the most beneficial and pleasant forms of gymnastics, because stretching, applying pressure and vibrating our body, cures and expands our physical perception. In fact, perceiving a little pain while doing this practice indicates which parts are the weakest, in need of treatment. This self-massage doesn't aim to increase muscle mass or physical performance, but to identify our weak points in order to strengthen them and maintain the whole body in shape. It is well-known that lengthening parts of the body strengthens them, but applying pressure, rubbing them and making them vibrate triples the benefits, since it facilitates the passage of energy, be it in the form of blood flow, nervous impulse or endocrine stimulation. It also promotes relaxation, firmness of bones, dispersion of toxins and evacuation. In fact, there is no part of the body that doesn't benefit from it. Any section of the body vibrates at a certain frequency when it is healthy, while when it is not, the vibration becomes irregular or disappears, in the same way oxygenation stops where there is no life. From this we can deduce that vibrations stimulate a part in difficulty. We are our own doctors. Moderation is always considered, and each of us must be aware of his or her limits. How do we know if our shoulders, knees, feet, tummy or head pains are of nervous, osseous or circulatory origin in order to treat them properly? Auto-massage works well for the majority of common ailments. Toxins that accumulate in some parts of the nervous system form something similar to a rigid sheath which prevents the nervous flow, dissolves with elongation, pressure, vibration. Appropriate pressure on a weakened bone structure speeds up the union between the two most important elements that make it up collagen, a connective tissue protein that acts as glue and calcium, the main structural element. Pressing the edges of a wound accelerates healing. After repeated tension, certain parts of the body could shorten, break, and then cause devastating effects. Mental and emotional flexibility must be maintained to prevent physical and mental ailments, relieve pain and impediments. We therefore need to train all our body parts, especially the nervous system, since it is the interlocutor in contact with the whole body. The nerves, cables charged with energy and data, comparable to violin strings or high voltage wires, must be elastic in order to be tuned and fulfill their functions. All altered body parts stiffen, swell, feel painful to touch and pressure. Tension in the neck and shoulders are the first to be noticed; but there are other less visible ones, for example, those in the heart, which behave in the same way but can be much more dangerous. Persistent tension can change all parts of the body, even the nerve endings that connect them, as they are not predisposed to the irregular passage of information or energy. Let's consider various symptoms: a heart under stress or trauma presents a surrounding painful area – a migraine alters vision and creates swelling and pain in the temples or in the upper parts of the orbital cavities – clogged bellies and intestines hurt if pressed – the electrocardiogram and the electroencephalogram perceive alterations of the nervous and circulatory systems with external sensors – the pace-maker, without being implanted in the heart, gives electrical impulses that control its rhythm. We therefore note that there is a connection between the internal and external parts of the body. Consequently: pressing, stretching and making the external parts vibrate can also affect the most important organs, such as heart, kidneys, stomach, intestines. Identifying and fighting pain through elongation, pressure, vibration, thus stimulates healing. This is the main reason why yoga, Shiatsu, Do-In, acupuncture, and thousands of massage versions are still in vogue. So, "do it-yourself" does it better because: we can decide how long and how hard to exert the pressure, we don't have to spend money, and we can immediately prevent and counteract ailments.

A gym to discover

Many of you will never have thought of it, but we all have a gym, ready for use and free, which allows us to carry out all the exercises necessary for our well-being: our home. In the kitchen, in fact, we can find a multitude of excellent "multi-functional gymnastic devices", for our daily training: the table, chairs, some furniture, doors, walls, bed, culinary equipment, a basketball, or football, a Rackatoy (a tool described at page 104) and much more.

Let's see together, room by room, what we could do in each of them.

THE KITCHEN

The best spa in the world. We eat, drink, watch TV, discuss, and rest in the kitchen. We can eat well or badly, argue and get angry, but also do something different, enjoyable and above all interesting. Here we will surely find a table, chairs, household utensils, a counter, a free wall, a floor... unlimited points of support to take advantage of our weight to stretch, compress, massage the whole body with minimal effort.
Starting with the chairs, we could use them to:

To release tension in the torso

In this way, the entire trunk, the axillary hollows, the shoulder blades and the arms are stretched.
The position is excellent for easing some heart, chest, and shoulder tension. Slowly sliding our arms on the top rail of the chairs elasticize the entire body structure, veins and surrounding arteries next to the pressured area.

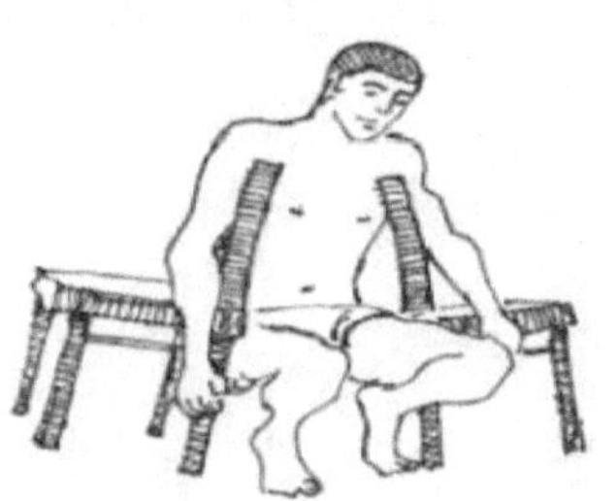

Variants: move the chairs slightly back to expand and rub the chest and other parts of the arms from different angles; move one or both legs forward; bend knees to strengthen the pelvis, knee, and feet; undulate, vibrate…

Consult a physician before undertaking any exercise. The pieces of furniture must be stable and sturdy and the tools solid; not too high or too low for the chosen exercise – Avoid proximity to glass, mirrors, carpets, and windows. Don't hang on pipes and beams; be careful not to slip, be aware of your limits. To soften the exercises, we can place a pillow or towel between us and the support points.

One of the most comfortable positions

As shown in the picture, while watching television or surfing the internet or reading a book, with only our body weight, our backs and knees stretch and strengthen. To increase safety, we use a sofa or an armchair instead of the chair and bring other chairs closer.
Variants: place calve muscles on top of chairs and then slide and vibrate them – put one leg on top of the other one to increase pressure – change the angle and position of support points.

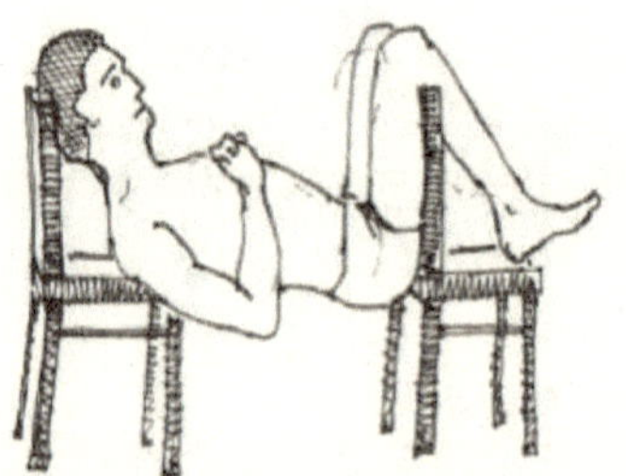

Only the dynamic (careful not to fall) and stronger, holding them- selves with their hands, can slip and arrive with their back on the ground to increase elongation and benefits.

Tensions, aches and pains, are subjected to: the law of attraction, the karma, like cures like, magnetism, as already seen in homeopathy, biology and toxicology. By stretching, pressing and vibrating, a moderate tension creates pain, but relieves tension and pain.

Raising the point of resistance strengthens and heals.

Stomach aches, constipation?

Consult a doctor before doing any exercises
Changing our diet is important, but we could try this exercise too.
(We should increase liquid intake with soups, teas, vegetables, broths...).
Swinging with our hands on the seat of a chair, and sliding our stomach, intestines, or bladder on the top of the chair stimulates evacuation. By moderately pressing the stomach while keeping the abdominal muscles relaxed, perceiving some pulsations, improves abdominal aorta elasticity.
This is a part of the circulatory system second in importance only to the heart that bases its efficiency on flexibility.
Remember to hold this position only for a few seconds.

We can compress the erogenous zones to increase their blood flow, improve the nervous response and stimulate spermatogenesis.

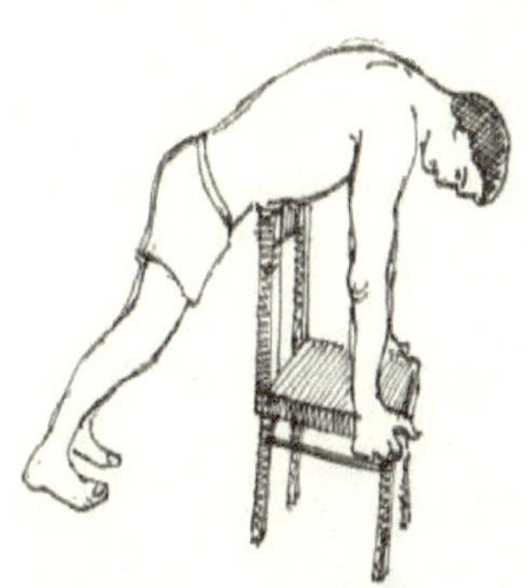

To vary the exercise we could also:
lean the chest on the backrest, sway, jump, swing, alternate the pressure on the body, change position on the support.

Knees and ankles

Above a chair we can: bend more than when kneeling on the ground, thus to raise the pressure in the upper part of the body – oxygenate the upper body better create the necessary space that allows the regrowth of knee cartilages – stretch the worn parts of our ankles and knees on the seat chair. Following the pain-pleasure sensation as a guide while bending, and slightly pressing the knees from different angles, favors the repositioning of the joint ligaments. The cartilage can do his job effectively only with a well-positioned joint. To heal our knees effectively, we could (consult a doctor) also: press them against the edge of a table or other piece of furniture to reposition them – put a rolling pin between the popliteal fossa and the femur, to pull them apart – put ourselves in the previous position " the most comfortable position" or with your back on the ground hook the popliteal cavities to the backrest of the chair, or to the Rackatoy – bend the knees whenever possible.

VARIOUS POSITIONS TO RELEASE TENSION

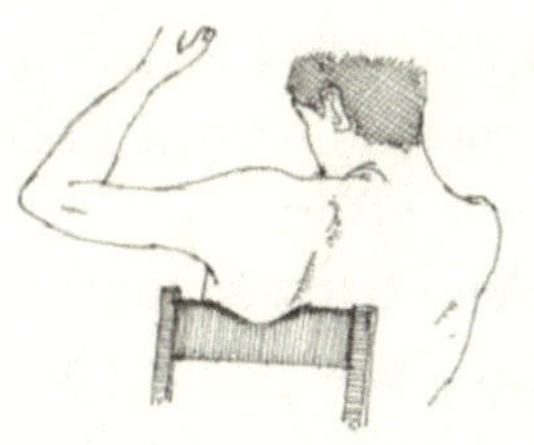

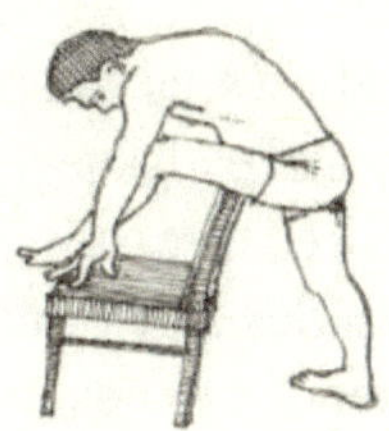

Pressing the shoulder blade against a chair while sitting relieves tension in the shoulders. To alleviate the tension caused by sciatica, we will stretch the leg more often and press the thigh as long as possible on the top rail of a chair. We can put ourselves upside down, to rapidly increase the pressure on the upper body, so to stretch the back and press the area adjacent to the erogenous zones and the intestine.

The herniated disc

Consult a doctor Besides eating, much more can be done on the dining table for health. Thinking about doing gymnastics where we eat can make us reluctant.

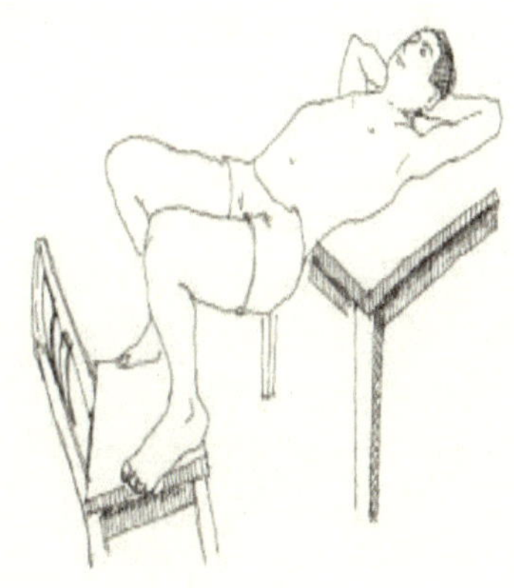

We have the subconscious idea that we should only eat on the table, that it is not suitable for doing something else, however, putting ourselves on a raised and rather large support surface has many advantages. It is certainly more hygienic than the floor and it allows us to do a multitude of particular exercises for the back.

This position is special for those who want to prevent or postpone some serious back problems.
Using the edge of the table allows us to specifically press vertebrae by vertebra and adjacent connective tissues, to reposition them in their original position, at the desired pressure without effort. To vary the exercise, we can shake our ankles to vibrate the entire lower body: legs, stomach, intestines and erogenous zones included – change the position of the chair and the leaning point of the back – place the calf muscles on the top rail of the chair…
It is a perfect position to meditate, we could dedicate it to people comprehension, to breathing exercises that clears our mind or to fixate in mind something...

Upper body circulation

Slowly sliding your arms over the edge of the table improves: circulation of veins and arteries in the arms – elasticity of muscles and nerve flow in the upper body.
In this position we can also stretch the neck, by leaning instead we will stretch the calf muscles and the back.

We should also stretch and slide all body parts, whenever: we are outdoors, in the gym, in gardens provided with exercise equipment – we find the proper pole, bar… Never forget your health.

Neck ache and cervix pain

A difficult position to do (only for the strongest). Grabbing our heads with our hands and levering on the table as shown allows us to effectively stretch the neck, strengthen triceps, dorsal muscles and axillary cavities; moreover, with minimal effort. To loosen stiff legs and toes, we change the support point and leg positions.

A flexible Back

By leaning on the table and rocking sideways, you can strengthen your entire upper body and stretch your back and the calf muscles.

Holding the breath in this position,
allows us to retract the belly to:
the maximum, swing, jump, vibrate,
stimulate energy flow, be it in the
form of blood flow, nervous impulse
or endocrine stimulation.

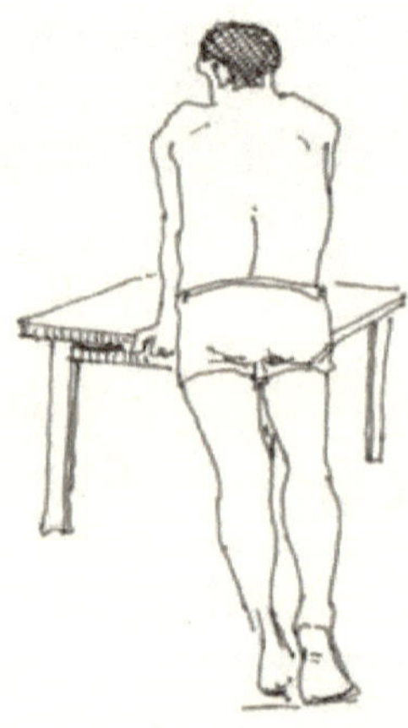

In this position we could also safely put one foot on top of the other to massage the instep and toes.

Upper body loosening

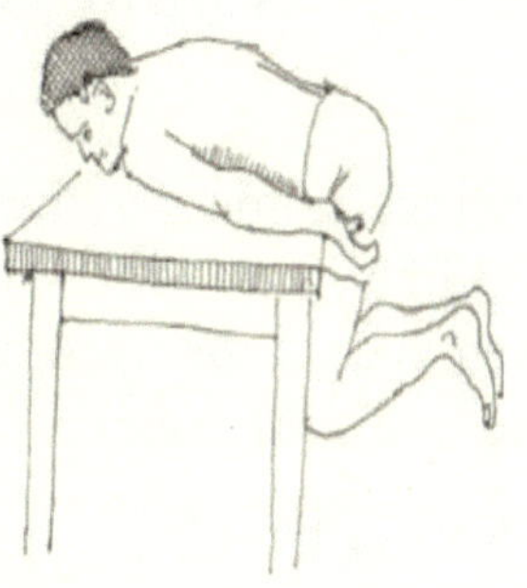

To maintain this position for a while or sliding the whole upper part of the body on the table, strengthens our chest, belly, intestines, and erogenous zones, counteracts face wrinkles, stimulates evacuation, as well as the nervous, circulatory and digestive systems.

Neck and shoulders

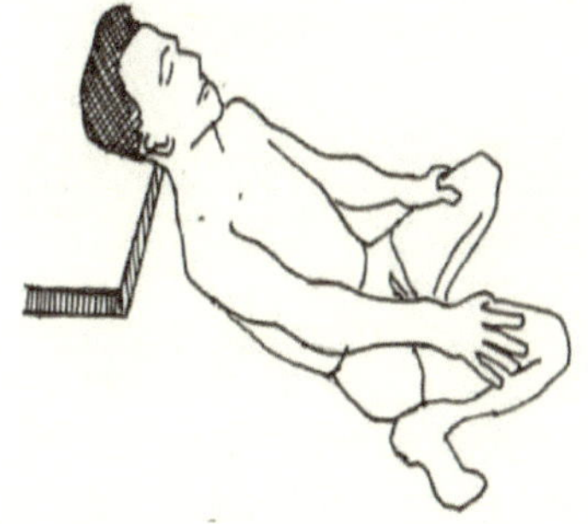

Placing the neck on the edge of a table or chair and turning the head sideways allows us to: extend more efficiently the whole neck, tilt, and effectively bend the feet and toes, compress the calves and thighs to favor circulation, extend the knees.

To strengthen the shoulders and stretch the back, we will support the whole body with the shoulder blades.

The sore spots guide the cure.
The pain does not usually go away on its own.

AEROBIC EXERCISES, AUTO-MASSAGE AND PLEASURE

Jogging, outdoor activities, sports should be common, but if we don't feel like it, or we can't go out for any reason, we could equalize and even exceed the benefits of various physical activities with this simple and beautiful exercise:

The backlash

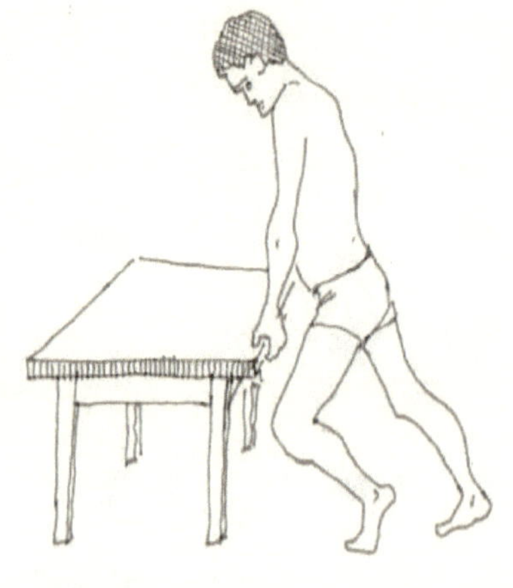

A suitable practice for everyone, even for the weakest and those who have impediments, since we decide which parts of the body we want to use and there is no need to implement any particular force. Leaning against a table and simulating a quick walk or jogging, is an excellent exercise for the circulatory system, but, if we interrupt the movement sharply with our hands on the table, the vibrations created counteract a fast heartbeat, stimulate emptying of the intestine and bladder makes us breathe forcibly by the upward shift of the diaphragm; and most beautiful of all: the vibrations awaken the reproductive system, to push us, thanks to the pleasure obtained to continue training. Vibrating stimulates circulation, oxygenation, the nervous system, the muscular apparatus…To vary: support surfaces of different heights are used, one pushes with one leg or both or with the hands; we jump, retract our stomach, intestines, make the pelvis oscillate.

The other advantages of this exercise, almost mandatory for lazy-intelligent people, are the strengthening of: several muscle groups: the shoulder girdle, the back, the pelvic muscles, the neck, and the legs.
For what concerns the cardiovascular system, regular exercise improves strength, and coordination of movement.

Compressing parts heals and strengthens them: Tuina, Shiatsu, Thai massage, Swedish, reflexology, physical-therapy... There are many wellness arts that rely on precise pressure points.

Taking advantage of the weight of the head alone, we can compress effortlessly painful parts of the hands and fingers to increase pain resistance and thus reinforce them.
This is one way to prevent the pain from recurring throughout the day, and even during sleep.

WALLS – DOORS – FURNITURES

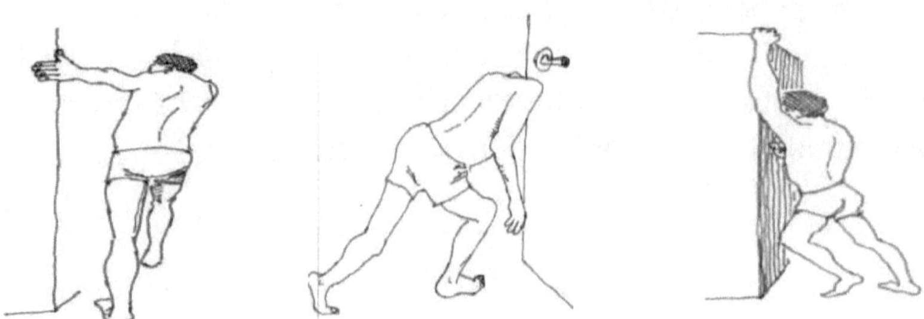

Pull – Push – Press

In the kitchen there is a refrigerator, a door, a wall, a counter… to be used to: hang on to stretch our arms, back and neck – press our forearms and shoulders, sideways too – lean the back curved against the corners – rub parts of the body otherwise difficult to manipulate – push every body part against.

We vary the exercises by: waving, floating, changing inclination, using some breathing techniques, and multiple support points at the same time.

THE ROLLING PIN

In the kitchen we can also find a rolling pin that will not only serve to prepare a cake or beat someone we know well. This culinary utensil, usually made of wood or marble of different sizes, due to its rounded shape, can also be used to massage our neck, feet, arms, legs and back.

With a rolling pin it is possible to gently drum, rub, and roll the whole body. A large one is used to massage the neck, back, belly and a narrow one to penetrate the popliteal fossa and tap various parts of the body like a tambourine.

A great way to tap with less effort is to drop the rolling pin several times on the desired area. Try to pass it (gently!) on the body or on the back of our spouse and children, and they will not let you stop.
It promotes blood circulation, nervous stimulation and gives pleasure.

The rolling pin and sciatica

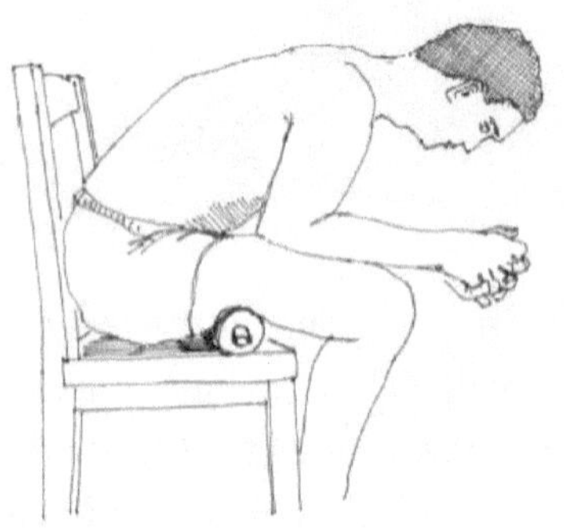

A chair and a rolling pin are the perfect combination to contrast sciatica. By placing one between the thighs and the chair and moving forward and backward, we receive a massage not to be missed, especially when some thigh muscle or sciatic nerve are tense.
Here with some creativity, we can make the exercise more sensual.

Rolling pin and feet

With a rolling pin under our feet, while we support ourselves firmly on a table, without tilting, in order to avoid falling, we can slowly swing back and forth to effectively rub our aching feet, get pleasure, and strengthen our arms. To stretch our toes safely, we will put a smaller rolling pin under them without tilting.

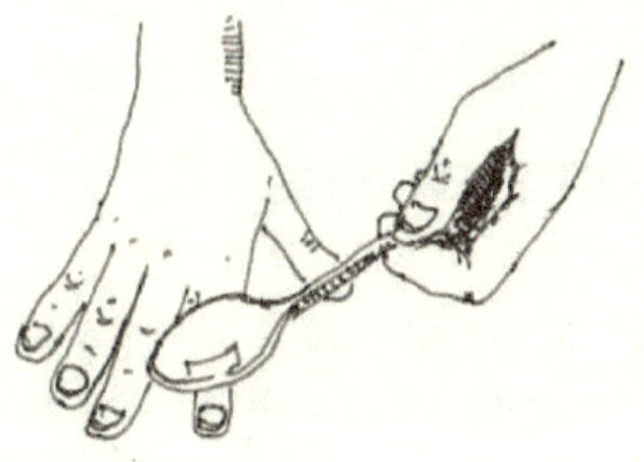

THE SPOON

Used as a drumstick to tap the most sensitive and weak parts, the metal spoon, for its weight and shape, is perfect for strengthening the fingers or some small painful points.
Just tapping a spoon can uncover hidden ailments, stimulate blood circulation, nervous response, and the union of collagen and calcium.

We tap any small area of the body to energize it, slither it on the skin to: get rid of superfluous fat, press its convex side with rotating movements on the wrinkles on the forehead, face, and the small reddish capillaries to stimulate blood flow, and in many cases to make them disappear.

A PERSONAL EXPERIENCE

All of a sudden, my little left finger, without having it in any way hurt or hit, started to bother me. Shaking someone's hand was hard, it seemed to be broken, it was so painful; what did I do then? I began to shake it, to press it, to roll it, with the other hand against the table, to tap it with a spoon for a while: it was slightly painful but also pleasant, so I continued; in the end, it was only a little finger, I could risk it, it was always aching anyway.

After a pretty long period of this "mistreatment", although rolling it, pressing it, against the table, it continued to creak, while the other fingers with the same treatment made no noise, the pain disappeared. Did I do something wrong? It doesn't seem so. Seeing is believing. One consideration: in Muay-Thai training the athlete throws powerful kicks against the bamboo; in some forms of karate and Kung-Fu athletes train to break sticks, to punch various materials, which gradually become harder and harder. The result?

They strengthen the muscles and also the bone structure since the impact creates micro-fractures which, by calcifying mount, bone density. From this we can deduce that we could (with much more delicacy and attention) do the same thing with a rolling pin, a spoon, a larger or smaller ladle to strengthen the femur, the shoulders, the kneecaps and many other parts of the body.

It is just a matter of vibrations.

THE MINI SAUNA

Consult a doctor before using essential oils, they are to be avoided during pregnancy, if you are an allergy sufferer, epileptic or have any medical conditions.

Although aromatherapy is not considered a real therapy, it utilizes medical elements and rules of use subjected to clinical and pharmacological studies. According to the theory, the use of essences would have: calming, expectorant, bactericidal, carminative... effects, depending on the oil used.

In the ancient world, aromatic woods were burned to ward off diseases, insects, and to worship their gods; the Egyptians were the first to develop essences, to discover their antibacterial and antiseptic powers and use them in the cult of the dead and the embalming. In modern times it is said that a researcher in the field of perfumes, after getting a burn, instinctively immersed his arm in the essence of lavender, and by drawing relief from it, began the search for their healing properties.

A doctor named Valet resumed his research and used that knowledge during the Second World War to treat wounds and disinfect enviroments. Later on, he completed his studies in the field by publishing a book entitled Aromatherapie which became famous. That is the event that launched the aromatherapy we are all familiar with today. In the kitchen we will certainly find some pots; taking one like the one shown above (to avoid using a towel), and heating some water to create steam to which we will add a few drops of essential oil, we will reproduce a mini sauna that can tone up many parts of the body.

Expectorating

Eliminating waste, toxins, chemicals… is beneficial for everyone.
The practice counteracts the damage caused by smoking and pollution, but to be more effective, we should also: before getting sick take some herbal teas – practice the deep breathing mentioned in the book and simultaneously vibrate the throat and tap the chest with our hands – do some physical exercise to stimulate sweating – be more in contact with nature: go to the beach and woods… and since water is the best purifier there is, to assume more liquids and foods that have a higher percent of it, can do only good to us.

Skin care

People with oily skin and acne are the first to benefit from it.
The water vapor keeps the skin clean and rehydrated, avoids wrinkles and slows its aging. After testing the pot edges with our fingers (water temperature very low), we could also press the skin face against them to grab a warm and gentle massage.

Relaxation

Slowly inhaling some relaxing oil and reflecting on everyday problems and stress causes, calms the mind, makes us feel better; we never do it enough, especially when we are down.

Eye care

Pay attention to the water temperature.

While inhaling we could: turn them to the left or right, up and down, form an eight with their movement and pull simultaneously the surrounding skin with the fingers, to strengthen the eyes nerve connections – keep our eyes open a little longer and stare at the oil or water bubbles to keep them moist and clean.

Method and ingredients:

A pot like the one shown in the picture – some essential oil – olive oil – optional towel – water vapor. Heat three or four glasses of water into the pot, to create steam – lower the heat – pour a few drops of olive oil into the water – add two, three, drops of essential oil on top of the oil drops, so as not to quickly disperse the essences – start inhaling.

We will alternate the practice with normal breathing.

Consider the moderation of the use and consumption of oils, three drops at a time for inhalation are sufficient. Repeat the operation at your discretion and use the instructions found in an aromatherapy book.

Inhaling water vapor can cause us to sneeze, cough, to expel mucus as if we had got a cold. Now the dilemma: are we sure that we must immediately take medicine to fight a cold, or it can be useful since in this way we get to read of nose and throat toxins? How many ailments come from the body's inability to eliminate waste?

Too many! When is a cold useful or harmful? If you have any doubts, consult the doctor.

Caution. Wash the pot often, the build-up of lime can create a hard surface that could break and produce small bursts that can cause burns.

INTO THE ROOMS

The bed is the ideal place for those who find the floor hard, cold or unattractive, have impediments or limitations; it is the most comfortable place in the house, the positions we use here are manifold: we could curve the back, stretch the feet, the neck, fight wrinkles, meditate, practice breathing exercises, massage yourselves and massage the members of the family. Physical contact and pleasure bring us closer to each other: here, especially if we think of Eros, the bed can be called the king of the house.

The neck supports the head, which is heavy, and then it has to bear a lot of confused information of the brain. Can't this be the reason why it is often rigid?

While lying comfortably in bed, pushing and turning the head slowly against the headboard of the bed to the right and left, or placing a rolling pin between the bed and the neck, relieves his tension. In bed, with our hands on the floor, we will strengthen the arms, increase the elasticity of the back and counteract wrinkles.

Letting the head swing increases its blood supply, which corresponds to nutrition and oxygenation in the most important parts of the body: the brain, the area around the throat, the pituitary, thyroid, hypothalamus glands…

The forgotten position

During the day we can stand or sit while working, playing, and discussing, or lie in bed while resting, reading, sleeping…
In addition to these positions, there is one in which we are upside down and should be practiced daily.
This is because the pull of gravity downwards is negatively reflected on the whole body:

- Varicose veins, sagging of the abdomen, wrinkles are visible external evidence, and let's not forget there is also an internal part underlying the same force.
- With the oxygenation capacity of the lungs and the pumping of the heart that worsen with the lesser cleaner air and advancing age, the most important glands shrink at a faster rate.
- When we are really sick or are out of breath, putting ourselves upside down and keeping our legs elevated, helps us quickly recover (even in the womb we are upside down).

Having had a heart attack, I would like to say that when I feel my heart tired, the inverted positions are mandatory to me.

The candle

The position is excellent for the whole body and should be done on the ground, but since we are often lazy, and it bothers us to go on the floor, a beautiful alternative will be to do it in bed. It elasticizes the spine, counteracts wrinkles, and promotes cerebral oxygenation. Variations: the legs are beaten against each other at the height of the thigh, calf and feet – the weight of the body is supported with an arm, to exert more pressure on the first lumbar vertebrae and pelvis – the legs are flexed back several times to stretch your back and neck – you lean your legs against the edge of a piece of furniture, a wall, to get other frictions.

The barrel

As shown in the picture, after breathing deeply a few times to recharge: we expand our chest to the maximum and compress it by pressing our knees against it – we hold the position for a few seconds – we breathe normally to recharge. We repeat the same procedure as we retract the chest and intestines.
The operation is to be repeated a few times; it is excellent for: increasing the elasticity of the respiratory and digestive systems, therefore to easily expel phlegm and toxins – strengthening the muscle groups involved in digestion and evacuation – elasticizing veins, arteries and organs – strengthening the arms – distancing the first lumbar vertebrae and the femur, from the tibia.

PERSONAL EXPERIENCE

Have you ever had sciatica?
Aches, pains, cramps that start from the back and reach the legs, and you cannot walk or sleep. The attacks can be sporadic but always intense, and their cause is often due to the crushing of the sciatic nerve by the lumbar vertebrae. An experience that we shouldn't forget when we complain about how things are going. It is considered a disease of the elderly, but I was certainly not old when it happened to me!
This means that this ailment happens to everyone and more often than we think. This should teach us that we must continue to learn to appreciate life; on the one hand, ailments can also serve this purpose: let's not forget these kinds of experiences, to analyze them and learn a lesson from them when something goes wrong.
Returning to sciatica, I remember I tried everything to counter it, but although everything seemed to be helpful, nothing was conclusive.
After several days of fighting, I surrendered and got two injections near the sciatic nerve. The problem was not solved, but at least I could sleep. After that, the sciatica disappeared, but the sole of the foot remained numb. I thought it wasn't so bad: I could walk and play. After some time, I went to play ping-pong with my son, and then started playing with someone who knew how to play well, so I got involved and started hopping, but after a few dribbles, I felt a strong blow to the right leg. Thinking that I had been hit in the calf with a bat, I spun around to defend myself, but there was nobody there. Convinced then that someone had thrown a stone at me, I looked for it, but there was no stone on the ground.

Only then I realized that there were no culprits, that I had suffered my first muscle tear. I could hardly walk, and I was limping. When I got home, I came to the conclusion that sciatica was the cause of the numbness and consequent weakening of the leg, which had caused the tear. After the accident, a radiological examination confirmed my deduction and spurred me to intensify the stretching exercises of the leg and trunk. I found that while before the tear some exercises with the Rackatoy were relaxing, after the tear, with the same exercises, the foot tingled pleasantly. I am convinced that this depended on the reactivation of the nervous flow. To conclude, I can say that, probably, thanks to my perseverance, sciatica has never reappeared, but I must admit that the foot has remained numb.

P.S. And what bothered me a few years later?
A couple of toes of the offended foot began hurting. To counteract the pain, I started stretching them, but I didn't get any satisfying results.
I did give up hope a little, but not my will to recover, so one day I did something different, I started to stretch persistently on a rail in a park, as I had never done before, the whole leg of the sore foot and the next day the unexpected happened: the toes that usually were sore in the morning didn't any longer bother me. The lesson I have learned from this experience is: you should never give up – when a part of the body aches, the cure is to be extended – there could be more to be taken into consideration – all ailments must be counteracted from several sides – maintenance is mandatory!

TO PREVENT SCIATICA

We can do a lot to postpone, prevent it, and reduce pain.

We can: shed excess weight (usually we always have a few extra pounds) – hang on the Rackatoy by the knee pits or armpits – stretch the back – sit with a rolling pin under the thighs – kneel with a rolling pin between the thigh and calf muscles – with the backs on the ground, hook a chair with the knee pits – stretch the legs with a scarf – press the thigh on the top rail of a chair, or on some railing, bar... (pay attention to its sturdiness and position) that we can find in some gardens, beaches... Every time we have the opportunity, we should carry out some maintenance, by stretching, pressing and vibrating, especially the weakened and painful parts of the body.

THE HANDS

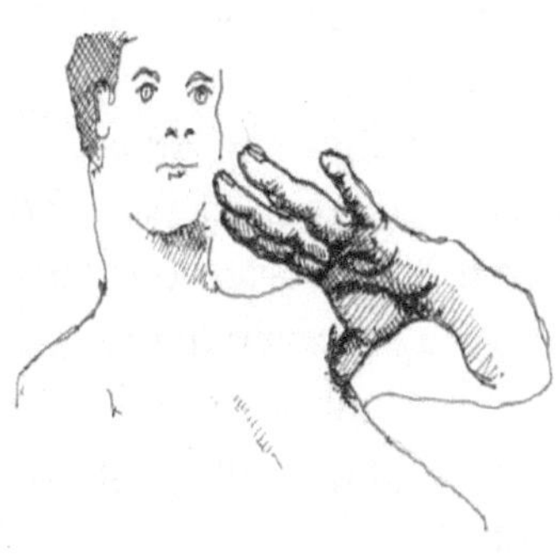

In bed we do so many things and so much happens.
Unfortunately, there is one thing that we never do enough of: we don't touch ourselves sufficiently; except for one part of the body, the others don't even seem to exist.

We have hands, and we don't use them when a simple touch could save our lives. We don't need to be experts; small pains indicate our weakest points. We should touch ourselves more often, press parts of the body and use various points of support, to find swellings and protuberances that could turn into serious illnesses. The doctors used to have the patients sit on a bed, look at their tongues, and palpate their bellies here and there – look for protuberances, pains in the liver and the stomach; any signal to identify hidden ailments. It doesn't take much for us to find with a touch or under some other form of pressure an enlarged or painful liver. We often eat and drink poorly, so massaging, rubbing, pressing, parts of the body every now and then, to find some changes should be a regular routine (consult a specialist), especially when they are aching. We can deflate the belly, stimulate the intestines, release tensions… By just observing a part of the body, we can discover anomalies, let alone feel them. The simple pressure of a thumb on a tense neck will loosen its stiffness, on one knee its swelling, on the armpit or chest, the tension of the heart…

By searching, we will find parts in need of care, and the perception of a mixture of pain and pleasure is the guide to find them and stimulate our own recovery.
How do we behave when a cramp takes us by surprise? Usually, we try to stretch the affected part, however, if we press its epicenter at the same time, we shorten our suffering. Try it, and then you will wonder why you have never made such a simple and effective action before. This is important because it proves that pressure relieves tension.
Let's remember, in this regard, to eat more bananas, which are rich in potassium, to increase the intake of magnesium and to regularly perform stretching exercises. Shiatsu, acupuncture, Do-In, and other techniques are based on this principle: pressure and touch. We can become experts because we always have a patient available at hand: ourselves! When a part of the body suffers, be it mental, physical or emotional, we must always go to the origin of the ailment to alleviate it.

The origin of the disease is always sought, be it mental, physical or emotional.

PERSONAL EXPERIENCE

I have treated many people with the Shiatsu technique.
I have massaged myself (Do-In), and I have also used my weight and different points of support to: effortlessly rub, stretch many parts of the body difficult to manipulate otherwise – learn to perceive those irregularities that stimulate healing. Similar to heartbeats, but too sporadic and close to each other to be confused with them, what are these irregularities and why does stimulating them help the part recover? If there is blood flow, there is also nerve flow, which should not be interrupted. I must say that these irregularities are not always perceivable by everyone, but they are yet additional proof that self-massage, massage as well as acupuncture are pillars of body care.

WE CAN RELEASE VARIOUS TENSIONS IN BED

On: the toes or a part of a leg by pressing or tapping a heel on them – the ankles, by curving them under the bottom – the calves, by pressing them against the knee or bending them and pressing them with your arms or heels – the fingers, hands and wrists by placing them between the hip bone and a rolling pin – the neck, arms, thighs, ankles, feet, in the following positions.

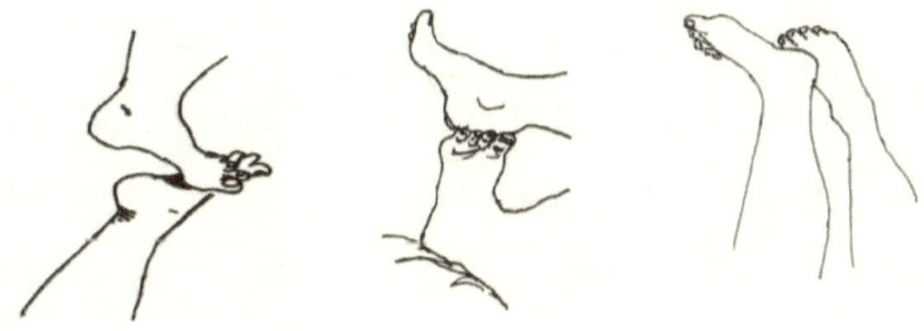

And we can do it by leveraging our body weight.

Neck tension will be released by placing our hands between our heads and the pillow. By pressing and tapping with your fingers or a spoon, a rolling pin, the chest, the axillary cavities, and several points adjacent to the heart, you will discover that the most sensible parts must be pressed more often, to release heart tension.

THE ROLLING PIN IN BED

While comfortably in bed we could do many things with a rolling pin. There are many ways of using one to stimulate the circulation, relieve and counteract the tensions, the constipation and intestinal swelling. Gently pressing, vibrating, the abdomen and intestines with our hands or a rolling pin is beneficial and also pleasurable.

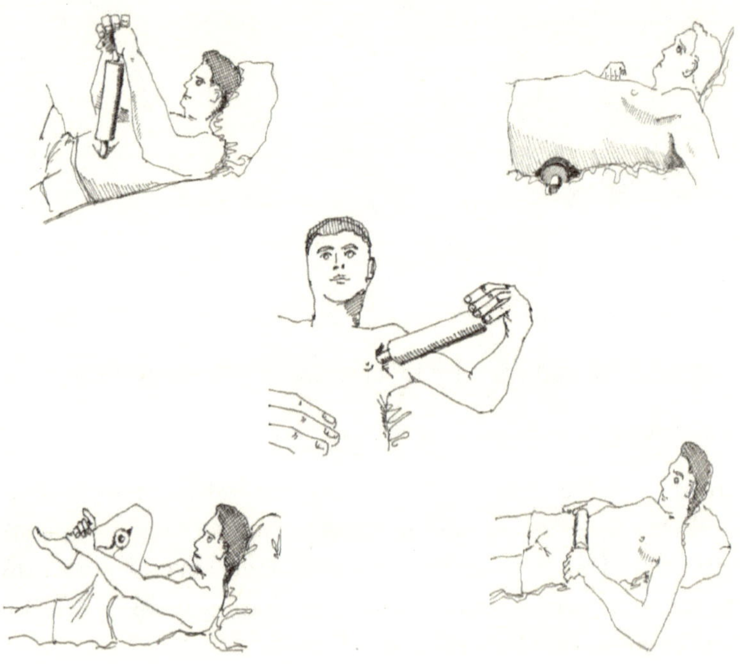

We can press many parts of the body without effort, by only resting our arms on the rolling pin. Since it is known that sleeping on a rigid mattress is beneficial for the back, and the whole body, we could put a rolling pin or a kitchen cutting board between the weakened parts of the body or the first lumbar vertebrae and the mattress to reinforce them and align our whole back.

THE BALL

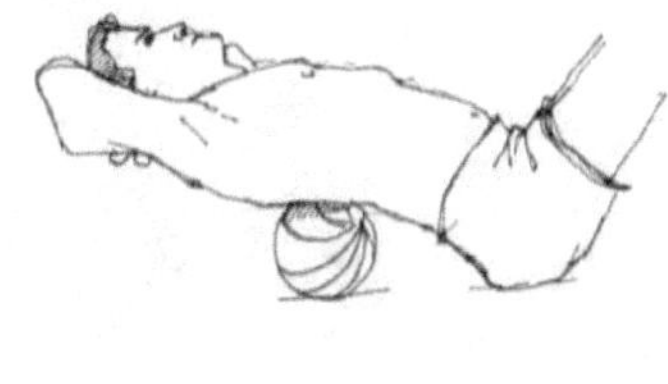

Balls are the indispensable objects of various games that can also be used for massaging ourselves. Small or large, and although not a modern invention, balls can still amaze us. With a leather basketball or soccer ball and only the weight of the body, we can effortlessly stretch and rub the neck, shoulder blades, back, pelvis, belly and erogenous zones; there is no part of the body that cannot benefit from it. Without any effort, we can roll the ball all over the torso, to receive pleasant frictions on the neck, and the entire back. We can use a ball to stretch out while watching TV, and we can even take it out with us to grab a nice outdoor massage and a tan at the same time.
With just our own weight, we rub the belly and intestines.

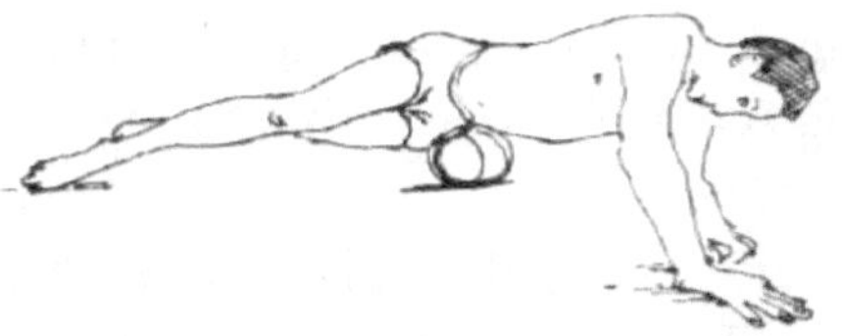

We compress the lumbar areas. Do you have shoulder pain? It could just be that our sleeping position is wrong, that we sleep with one arm under the body. The posture should be corrected, and the ailment counteracted by: placing a rolling pin between the shoulder blades and the mattress – rolling a tennis or baseball ball between the shoulder blades and a wall or floor – pressing the painful part against a piece of furniture – tapping the part with a rolling pin or a ladle…

A BELT FOR THE BACK AND HIP

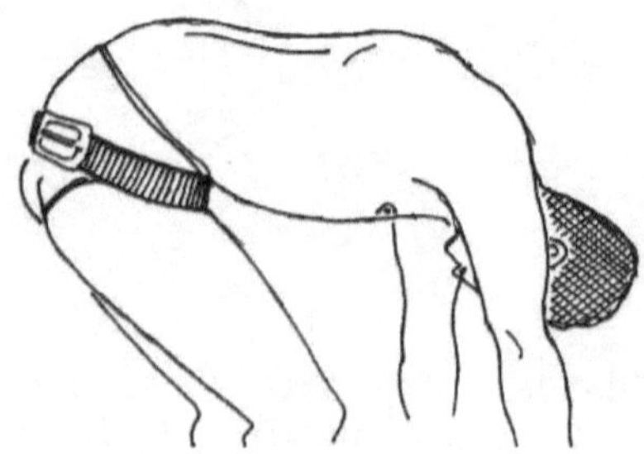

Due to aging and the effort to support the entire upper body weight (65% of men while 35% of women, most likely because their pelvis is more robust to sustain pregnancy), sooner or later the first lumbar vertebrae give up. We can prevent and postpone this decay by losing weight, with targeted stretching exercises and by wearing a common belt used in weight lifting.

In this way, leverage on the belly will relieve strain and pain to the lumbar area. The same belt is also excellent for strengthening the hip cartilages. By tightening it around them and bending the bust forward, or going with it around the house, we massage the hip and stimulate cartilage repositioning (consult a doctor if you have had surgery in the area). To complete the treatment and counteract (consult a doctor) the weakening of the femur, we could, while comfortably in bed: lean the femur and hip on a rolling pin, press the parts against a piece of furniture, a wall, tap the painful part with our hands, a ladle, a rolling pin… Everything to stimulate through vibrations, pressure and elongation: blood and nerve flow, relocation of the articulation, the union of calcium and collagen and toxins dispersion.

Pain is a warning sign that tells us that something is wrong and we should do something about it.

AILMENTS COUNTERATTACK IS DONE FROM MORE SIDES

We can counteract physical, mental and emotional ailments with: targeted gymnastics, herbs, supplements... Consult a doctor.

To strengthen cartilage and bones

We could:

- Do targeted gymnastics, consume nettle and horsetail herbal teas, apply poultices of these two herbs or cabbage on the affected part, alternate hot and iced water to stimulate circulation on parts of the body in need of attention...
- Assume the cartilage of the skate and the bones of the cuttlefish, to take calcium and collagen supplements in their purest and most natural form; both are used in supplements.

The bones of the new cuttlefish are rich in calcium and phosphorus, melt in the mouth and are easily digestible.

The skate is part of the cartilaginous fish and its bones, the cartilages in fact, are rich in collagen and proteoglycans, the elements that make up every cartilage. After eating the fish, in order to easily digest the cartilage, you choose the finest and most tender parts to store.

Few grams a day are eaten away from meals accompanied by a nice lemonade.

Consult a book that delves into the use of medicinal herbs.

TOOTHPICKS AND SKEWERS

People who have suffered heart trauma should seek medical advice. Skewers are excellent for making meat, vegetables, fish or fruit dishes and also suitable for scratching, rubbing, drumming and grasping parts of the body to reactivate the nerve and blood flow.
Used in Japan by some Geisha for a valuable erotic massage and by various Shiatsu operators to diversify the pressure and the effect of the massage, skewers are the progenitors of acupuncture. Paying attention not to hurt yourself, they are a special scratching tool for those itches that we can't reach and beg to receive. Fingers, the edges of pieces of furniture, tables, balls, the Rackatoy… Each object used to exert pressure on our body will make us feel different sensations.
Toothpicks in particular, at certain specific points, will cause some unique perceptions (without bleeding (•́ ‿ •̀).

Like a dowser who finds water thanks to a divining rod and his intuition, a small toothpick in the right place might astound us: seeing is believing.

PERSONAL EXPERIENCE

I have practiced auto-shiatsu on myself (Do-In) and many people, and although I am not an acupuncturist, at a time when I was worried about my irregular heartbeat, while imagining the first tools used in acupuncture could have been stones or sharp bones, I began to gently press a toothpick on the parts of the chest that I already knew were sensitive to touch. Using only the pressure of a finger, I searched here and there, and after several attempts, I felt some points of the chest, unlike others, were almost electric: one for example caused an intense sensation that made me stop pressing. The experience was certainly unique, and after a while the arrhythmia disappeared. It has been scientifically proven that various pressure points on the body promote the release of adenosine, a compound of adenine that has pain-relieving properties and assists in the regulation of heart rate and sleep. However, it would be risky to say that just some poking solved my arrhythmia, since, at the same time, I tried to remain calm, I took hawthorn and chamomile, I avoided coffee and alcohol, and in addition I countered the fast beats by practicing the backlash, (an original exercise described in this book), deep breathing, and I put myself in the candle position. In any case, all this confirms that doing-it-yourself really works.

Pressure causes tension and pain, but a controlled pressure relieves tension and pain.

THE SCARF

While lying in bed, with a scarf we could stretch individually or simultaneously our backs, legs, neck, toes.

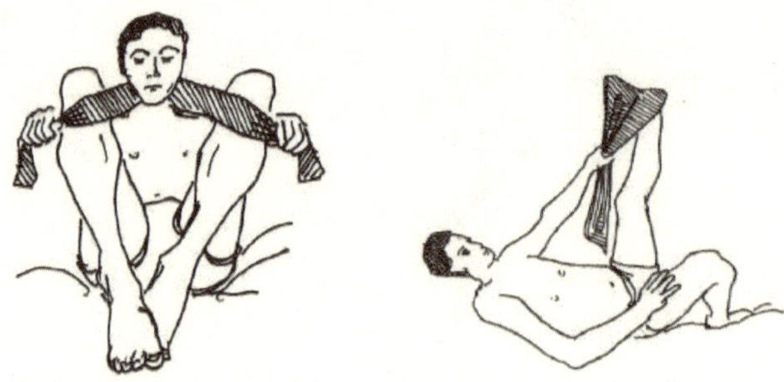

By pulling its ends and moving the scarf back and forth, we will be able to massage various parts of the body.

Leveraging on the body and our rigidity, with the two ends of the scarf tied together, we will pull all our body effortlessly.
With a little imagination, there is no part that does not benefit from it.

AND OUR EYES?

Have we ever thought about them? We are always in front of the cell phone or computer, and as a result, our eyes get tired.

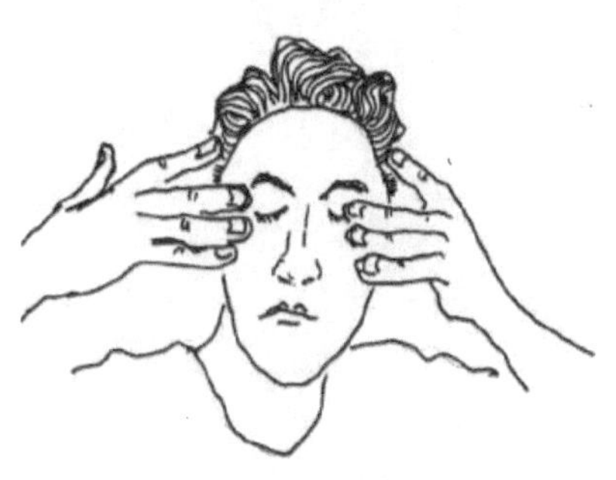

They need maintenance just like every other part of the body, and gymnastics and self-massage are methods to recharge them and prevent their quick deterioration. Here are a few ideas to cure the most important of our five senses.

We could: look far and then close – squeeze them gently with your fingers – keep them pressed for a few seconds with the sole force of the eyelid muscles – close and turn them in all directions while pulling the eyelids with the fingers – massage them – pull the eyelids up with the fingers as we try to close them with the only force of their muscles – tap them lightly with the fingers – every time we make a chamomile or tea, put the, still warm used bag on them. And we should let them rest whenever possible.

AND OUR SKIN?

We want to be beautiful and often forget that: the aromatherapy proposed is excellent for the skin face – you should prefer food rich in water – we are often overweight – exercise is mandatory – to capsize counteracts the force of gravity…

There are many factors that contribute to beauty, to the slowing of aging and among these, it often escapes us that we have two hands that can be used to massage and tap all our body. We will do it with oils and cosmetic creams, and to nourish and refresh the skin, whenever we eat aloe vera, avocados, bananas, coconuts, walnuts, watermelon…

The pulp or peel of many fruits are the best and less expensive natural creams.

IN THE BATHROOM

Water has always been a precious element and will become increasingly so: without it we cannot exist. In many places on the earth there is no water, in others it only comes occasionally, or there is none.
Somewhere, we have to go and get it, or even better, it is contaminated, and we may even die because of it. Where there is enough water, even if you sometimes pay for it dearly, its harmonious beauty and the benefits it gives us are too often underestimated: a nice shower, a hot bath, aren't perhaps among the greatest pleasures we can give ourselves every day?

A tribute to water

How long can we remain without water at home? If the flow of hot water, delivered by an intermittent shower head on the body, or immersing yourself in a hot, warm or cold bath relaxes you, makes you feel good, then the water is truly precious: we must appreciate it and use it sparingly. *Only when we recognize something precious, we appreciate it; only at that point we are thankful and consequently happy.* In the bathroom we could: bend over and offer the back to the jet of water and simultaneously obtain a massage to the back area – stimulate the internal organs, through its only pressure; rest our head and neck or press our shoulders, backs, legs against the shower wall, and let the water flow to manipulate and energize them. With our eyes closed, turned towards a weak sprinkle of water, we can gently massage the most important sense of the body. A hydro-massage shower or a Jacuzzi are extraordinary self-massage tools. Directing a jet of water can friction a weak and aching part of the body and give us an immediate sensation of well-being. Relaxation, better circulation, cleansing of the skin and respiratory system are benefits of water and steam pressure.

In the bathtub *Attention: bathtub, shower, and sauna must be well ventilated.* With your face just out of the water, letting your head float with only your nose and mouth out of the water, making a little noise with your mouth as we exhale, it will make us perceive, through the vibrations of the water, a sound which will transform the bathroom into a relaxing meditation.

Water is the inner and outer purifying element par excellence

THE RACKATOY

Consult a doctor before initiating any exercise. Beware: animals and children nearby may jump on you during stretching exercises, do not let the little ones play alone with the tool – to become familiar with the tool start playing with the lowest rungs – any exercise that you are unable to do with or without the tool, may indicate local or general weakness – consider your limitations – the Rackatoy must be firmly attached to the ceiling or the wall; the maximum capacity per set of rungs is 100 kg.

For children it is a swing, a trapeze, a toy; they can do so many things with it. If we whistle or sing the classic song that announces the arrival of the circus, they immediately become clowns or trapeze artists who prepare to jump. They play, have fun, and also do corrective gymnastics: the best for their posture and development.

The Rackatoy promotes interaction between adults and children, between children and also among adults. It's a portable gym that can be used in a simple and fun way. It is possible to experiment, standing or comfortably lying on the ground, stretching and relaxation exercises essential for health. It is: an ideal tool for self-massage, a flexible small Swedish square and wall bars, a swing, a body press, and a game for everyone. With the advantage of the support points that adapt to each person's conformation and that it can be personalized, with only our weight, we can relax, stretch, compress, rub, the entire body with pleasure and without effort. It is suitable for everyone, young, old, injured and expressly for intelligent lazy people. So let's choose the best place in the house to place it, and let's learn, in order to conclude this reading with beauty, in which ways we can use it for our well-being.

Best massage chair, there is no better way to relax

In these two very comfortable positions, by dosing the traction to our pleasure and exploring the countless variations, we can relax and stretch the whole body with no effort.
We may vary these positions by sliding on the lowest rungs and leaning on the ground, swinging....

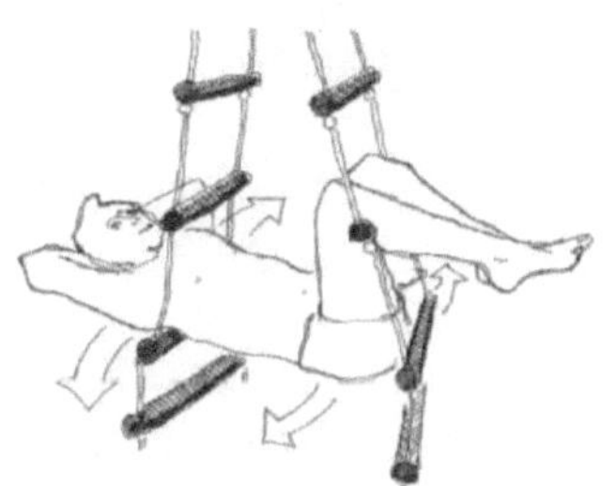

To avoid or postpone surgeries

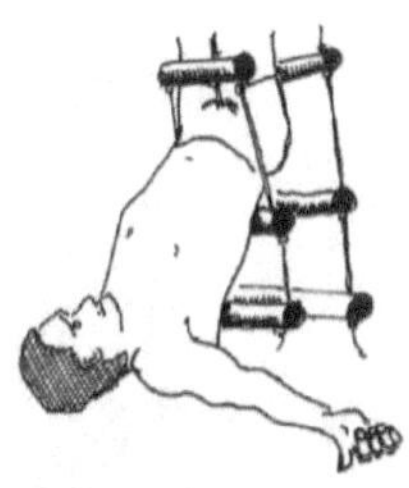

In these two positions, we are able to apply pressure aimed at distancing the first lumbar vertebrae: the area of the back that undergoes more surgeries than any other part of the body.
To see some exercises with tool, visit the you tube site: espressioni di guarigione https://youtu.be/MoZntupb3Gw

There is no better way to relax at no cost

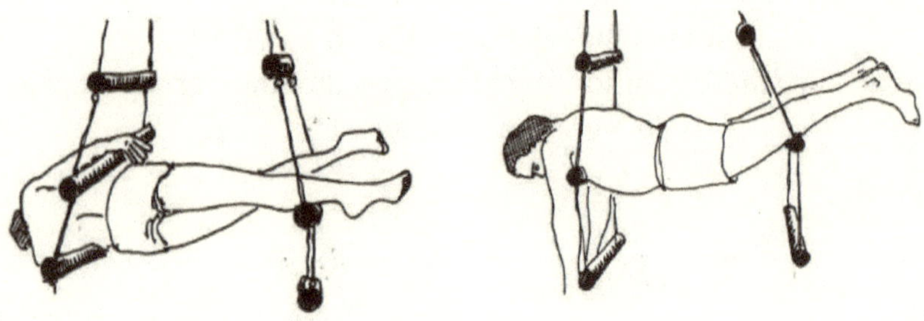

It has never been easier to stay upside down

With our back leaning on the floor, in this position, we can hang upside down for a long time. It is one of the best methods to effectively oxygenate the entire upper part of the body. The neck, ankles and torso get an excellent stretch, and if we sway, we receive, as in all other positions, a pleasant massage.

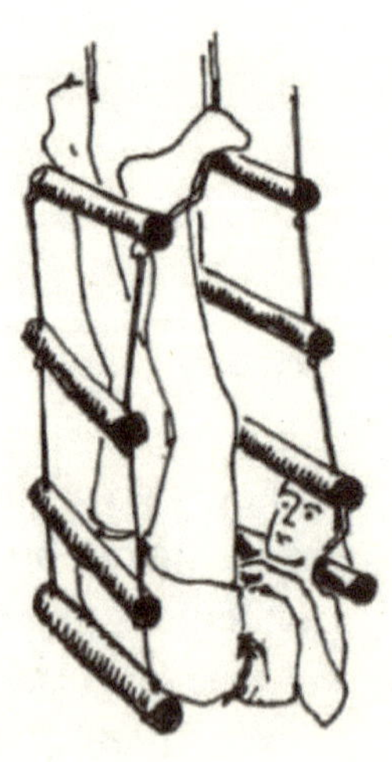

Stretches for any gymnastic practice

Various positions allow us to stretch countless parts of the body. The tool can also be used to enhance, vary, facilitate: yoga, shiatsu, many types of gymnastics, martial arts, love connections, etc.
It serves perfectly as an "aid tool" to massage others, too.
The Rackatoy is versatile: the elderly and the weakest people can use it to support themselves with their hands and body while doing some exercise. With the help of the rungs arranged at various heights, they will be also able to lower and get themselves up without anyone's help.

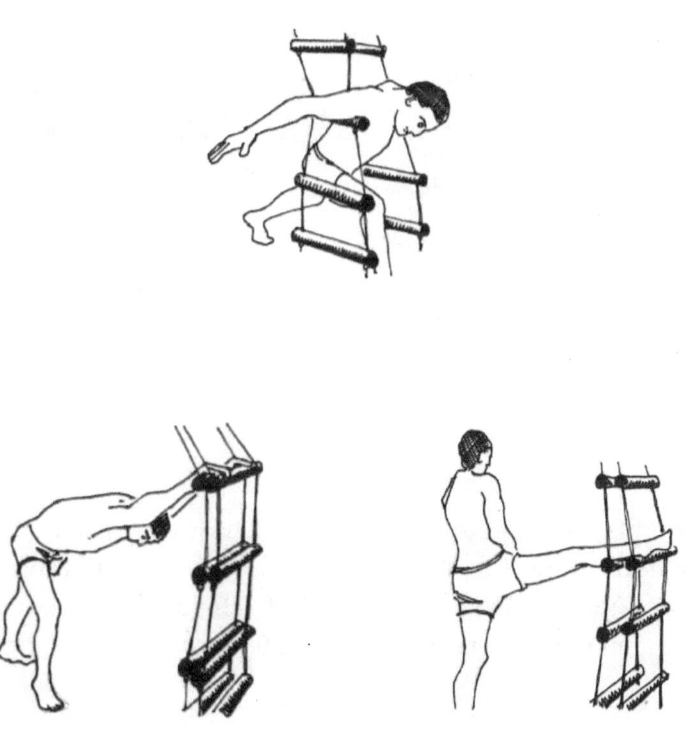

Muscles

There is no part of the body that cannot be reinforced with this tool. By only exploiting our own weight, we can do strenuous exercises that will make us gain muscular mass.

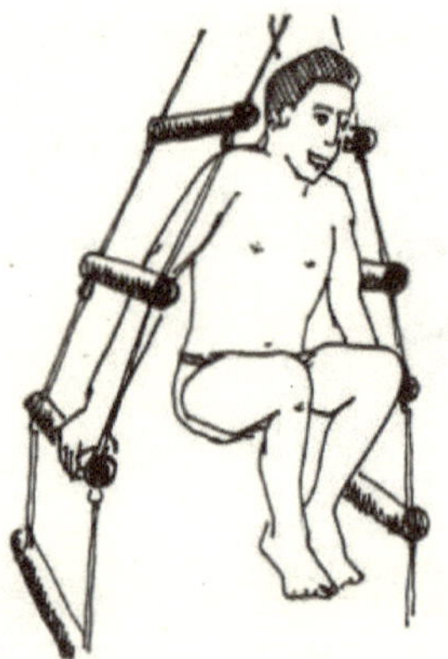

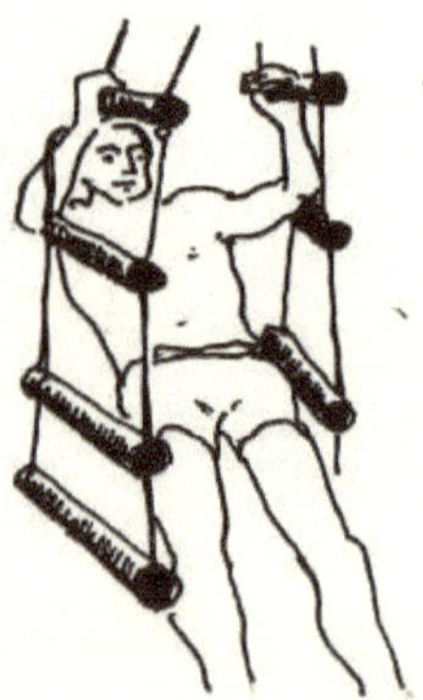

Other benefits of weightlifting with Rackatoy are: increased strength and bone mineral density, improved posture, endurance, cardiovascular health, appearance, blood pressure, HDL cholesterol, maintenance of weight loss, and most importantly: all with a lower risk of injuries.

The rowing machine

Joining two pegs and sitting on them, then pushing any of the pegs in front of us will transform the Rackatoy into a sort of rowing machine which will strengthen our biceps, triceps, abs, with only our body weight as a counterweight.

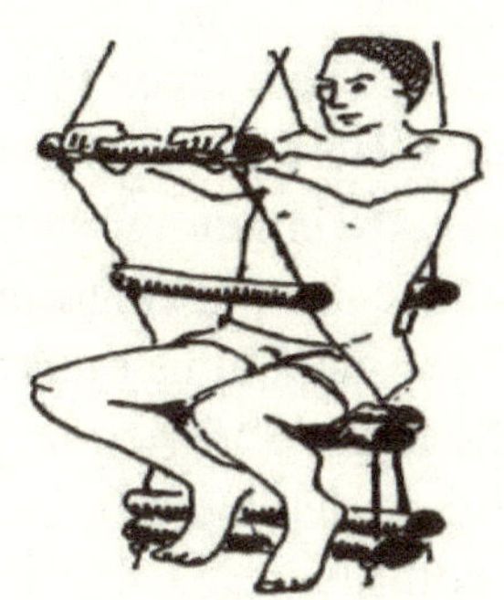

The Rackatoy is multi-functional: we can use it as a press to stretch the neck and compress the arms and legs.
A game, a gym and a masseur, all at hand, always available.

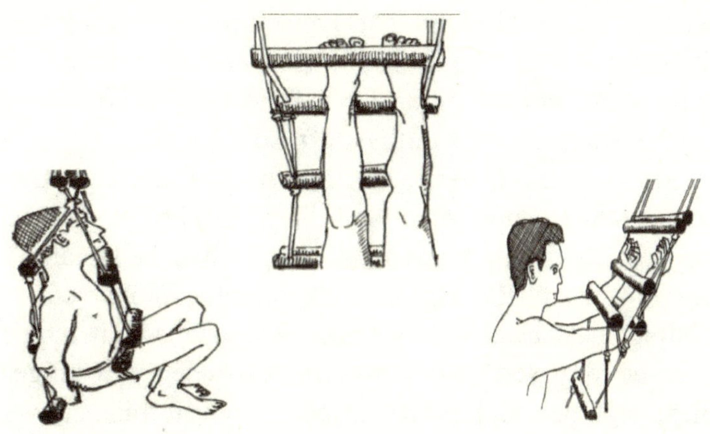

A smaller version of the tool can be positioned above the bed to allow the disabled to entertain themselves and exercise too.

A NOD TO NUTRITION

After having dedicated most of my life to the restaurant business as a chef-owner, I couldn't avoid sharing something interesting in the field of nutrition. The kitchen is a place that often takes us off the path to our well-being. Here forgetting all good intentions is very easy; it is almost impossible to remain vigilant, with temptation always lurking.

Exercising comes to mind only when we are forced to lose weight. In the kitchen, most of us think: "what are we going to eat?"

Food is energy, and we are greedy for it. What is more important than feeling good, having a full stomach and raising our morale? By eating, we temporarily reach this goal, thus we end up eating too much, and gluttony with various associated pathologies prevails over health. There are more people dying of diseases related to abundance than starvation. We forget how young and slender we were. We cannot stay forever young, but we should at least stay slender to avoid ailments.

There aren't many overweight octogenarians around; therefore, to increase our lifespan, we should be thin and agile, whether we like it or not. Losing weight is ideal and harmonious for all living beings. Better eating habits make us live better, longer, and save natural resources. We could start looking into the refrigerator, in it, we can find everything: healthy and unhealthy stuff, sources of energy or ailments. What we find in the refrigerator reflects who we are and how we treat ourselves; it outlines our habits and the possibility of reaching an old age. The best food that helps most people live better and longer is definitely not meat. Raising animals requires more resources than crops. Eating meat causes drowsiness, sluggishness. It requires more energy to be digested; we consume less energy to digest fruits, vegetables, legumes and grains. Meat is not forbidden, we live in different places, and we are not all the same, but lowering its consumption is beneficial for everyone, as we usually eat too much of everything, and especially of it. Perhaps we should only eat animals that have completed the cycle of life worthily and take a step back in time in agriculture to return to work the land with animals and fertilize everything naturally.

The quality of vegetables and life of animals, and consequently that of humans would certainly be improved. The refrigerator gives irrefutable proof of what is worthwhile ingesting to live longer. Let's try to leave the refrigerator closed for a week or two, and what will we notice?

Some foods rot faster than others.

Meat and fish will be the first to deteriorate, but we will prefer eating wild fish because of fewer treatments.

Aged cheeses maintain well because they are dry and salty, while those fresh do not keep well due to the greater quantity of water contained; both are to be evaluated because they are rich in fat, protein and high in cholesterol and calories.

Their consumption, as for all other foods, depends on the daily caloric intake. Butter will keep as well as all fats, perhaps because cows like pigs, by creating irresistible and harmful products, take revenge for the loss of the calf and their death. Even if we know very well the imbalances that animal fats cause to the body, most of us will never say no to butter or fatty products.

Yogurt keeps well and will be evaluated for the lactic ferments that promote digestion. Eggs keep well refrigerated and not.

Although we usually exceed the protein intake, given: their digestibility, the usual number of eggs ingested (compared to a steak or cutlet size), and the inferior treatments to which they are subjected: antibiotics, medicines… their consumption should be increased.

We should avoid cured meats because they tend to be fatty and with-stand decay only thanks to preservatives. We will prefer prosciutto because drying is the main element that preserves it. Pasteurized milk should be taken into account for the vitamin D, but kept under control not for the milk itself since it is too often combined with: snacks, biscuits, chocolate, foods rich in fats, sugars and preservatives.

Considering ice creams, snacks, chocolate bars, desserts, and various sauces such as mayonnaise and many ethnic foods that we believe are low-fat or sugar-free, we always exceed the daily calorie intake.

Someone will prefer milk to eggs or fish, but the calories intake should always be evaluated, and all sugar related foods banned from every table, since they, too often do more harm than meat, fats, and preservatives. In the end, which food wins the battle against decay? Vegetables, legumes, seeds, tubers, cereals, the least manipulated by man. In the refrigerator cabbage and kale are kings, carrots and celery are Queens and princesses, tomatoes and salads are counts and barons, eggplant, zucchini and spinach generals, watermelon and grapes commanders… In the pantry we should also find: dried mushrooms, onions, garlic, bananas, oranges, lemons, apples, potatoes, pumpkin ginger, flax and sunflower seeds, walnuts, almonds, pine nuts, herbs… all bastions of health that store well even outside the refrigerator and in the heat. There is no better, and they should never be missing or get rotten because we do not use them. Considering that some foods keep longer, won't that be a good reason to believe that increasing their intake makes you live better and longer? Where are the best antioxidants found? In fruit, vegetables, roots, seeds and herbs. Where do we live most? In various parts of the world where people prefer a vegetarian diet and the consumption of wild fish – where less meat is eaten – in quiet areas where there is no war and the air is cleaner.
What should we eat more of?
Even if we know what we should eat, for various reasons, it is difficult for us to do so. Infusions, herbal teas, extracts, roots, seeds… are often considered only when we are sick. Why not use them before? They contain: mineral salts, antioxidants and organoleptic properties, they are calming, detoxing, antibacterial, laxatives, energizing… Losing weight and having better eating habits, it is difficult to do.
Even if we know full well the advantages of a healthy diet, we fail to implement it because health is not in the foreground, we never value our time quality: the element that corresponds to health but is more practical to keep in mind.

Fasting

All the most important religions give great importance to fasting: Lent, Yom Kippur, Ramadan… Even today, doctors who integrate alternative medicine to modern ones recommend it for purification purposes. At this point it can be added that various studies on the intake of calories and fasting have proven that (known since ancient times) by abstaining moderately from food (it is not a question of starving, but of eating better and far less), cells, to supply themselves with energy consume everything they find: excess fat, toxins, waste, bacteria… entities that speed up aging. More recent studies claim that fasting before chemotherapy strengthens healthy cancer-fighting cells. In short, fasting has various advantages: we rejuvenate because it detoxifies – it reinforces the mind because dedicating attention to our healthy diet develops awareness and self-control – it puts materiality in the background.

Aren't these good reasons to eat less and better? Some examples of the benefits of fasting have come to us since ancient times: Jesus, Moses and Elijah fasted for 40 days. Pythagoras was sure that it helped the mind. Plutarch argued that fasting was better than any medicine.

Avicenna prescribed it as a cure for all ills. Isn't it true that too many times we get sick because we are clogged?

Aren't the lungs when they can't expel phlegm? Isn't the heart when it doesn't pump blood effectively because the circulatory system is clogged with cholesterol? Isn't the brain full of negative thoughts that cause it to go haywire or into depression (migraines are their fruit)?

Isn't diabetes a chronic disease characterized by an excessive amount of sugar in the blood? The intestine becomes clogged…

Animals are intelligently inferior beings with a higher instinct that avoid eating when they are sick.

SOME IDEAS FOR A HEALTHY DIET

Gianpaolo's tea

A recipe of a seventy-two-year-old man who attributes his fabulous shape to a meal a day and a lot of tea drinking.
A lemon tea with honey is an excellent method to purify our body.
To prepare the herbal tea, just boil the water, pour it over the herbs, wait five minutes (timing depends on the herbs used), pass the mixture through a colander, and then add a generous amount of honey and lemon juice. To lose weight and maintain a good shape, we will drink at least a liter and a half of it per day.
What are the physical benefits of this method? The stomach, due to the high nutritional power and digestibility of honey (it must be drunk slowly because it is food), and the quantity of water ingested, since it would not dilate, decreases its size and consequently the appetite.
A surgical technique shrinks a part of the stomach and gives the same results… Wouldn't it be better to drink a lot of tea?
Needless to say, after having finished the tea, hunger immediately takes over, everything becomes tastier, and overeating is not at all difficult. To avoid gorging, we will ingest something healthy and low-calorie, before hunger takes over.
The method is practical and effective because making a tea is simple and as long as we drink, we do not get hungry. One should remember not to eat anything else while drinking the tea, since honey is very rich in nutrients, and it would paralyze the digestion of other foods.

AVOIDING OVEREATING

It is difficult to eat little for various reasons: we do it out of nervousness, to release tension and for the pleasure of taste, so in the evening, after dinner, we start, for example, to nibble a piece of cheese and drink a glass of wine. Then the cheese is taken back and then the wine to push down the cheese, and so on, until there is no more cheese or wine. Then we end up being a bit tipsy, we forget the good intentions and move on to chips, chocolate, ice cream... Instead, munching pumpkin seeds will avoid eating too much and limit the damage of the abundance. To put something under our teeth, we will have to clean the seeds with our hands and mouth, which, due to time-consuming, we ingest rather little. Pumpkin seeds are not just food, they are rich in zinc, polyunsaturated fatty acids, vitamin A, E protein, and have a good percentage of iron. They prevent arteriosclerosis, lower cholesterol, hair loss, prostate problems, are suitable for people who have anxiety attacks, mood swings and have an anthelmintic action: they are toxic to tapeworms. Including them in the diet will help us cut cold cuts, cheeses and sweets. We will eat them before the appetite sets in, but let's not forget that they are quite caloric.

SOUP

Always different with just a few ingredients.

One way to support their integration is to prepare a nice soup more often, it will help us lose weight and at the same time ensure a higher dose of fluids, vitamins and minerals. To integrate it into our habits, the preparation must be fast, undemanding, possibly economical, and above all tasty. To speed up the base: garlic, onion, leek will be browned with olive oil, prepared once a week and kept in the refrigerator (they keep very well) or frozen.

We will consider that there are no mandatory ingredients: we will use what we find in the pantry. To prepare our healthy soup, we could use the base and just add: a little nut or light soy sauce and water, fresh or canned tomato or tomato paste, some herbs – onions and mushrooms or spinach – cabbage or green beans and some other vegetables – dried peas or lentils, mushrooms or just canned beans… Try experimenting with just one or two vegetables, you can get excellent results. To save money we will use the vegetables that we find cheap in the market, and to further speed up the preparation, we will cut the vegetables coarsely and then blend them with an immersion blender.

To flavor, you can add a mix of spices such as Curry, Masala, Cajun, turmeric or ginger at the beginning of cooking, or Genoese pesto, oregano, cumin and chili powder at the end. We will not forget: cheeses, Ajvar, Marmite, or sunflower, pumpkin and sesame seeds, the exotic or spicy sauces that we can find in supermarkets or ethnic shops. To be valid, the soup should be the main meal of the day, and will not include potatoes or cereals.

We will eat foods rich in carbohydrates separately because a good plate of spaghetti with tomato sauce or “pasta fagioli”, an Italian soup with beans and pasta, has no equal.

The healthy concoction is especially indicated to be prepared as a drink version to keep in a thermos and have it available throughout the day: warm in winter and cool in summer, like the honey-rich tea suggested before.

The leftovers can be re-cooked with other vegetables and seasonings, to save money and savor a new soup. In Ireland, there is a place where they serve a concoction known as the centennial soup because new ingredients have been continuously added to its leftovers for over a hundred years.

I hope your soup reaches the hundred-year milestone too.

FAST AND HEALTHY DISHES

Spinach or raw mushroom salad

Mixed together or separated, dressed with olive oil, lemon juice, flakes of Parmesan cheese and pepper.

Middle Eastern Salad

Diced peppers: green, red, yellow, cucumber, tomato, Feta cheese.

Fresh Tomatoes and Anchovies

Mozzarella and white onions are optional.

Caprese Genovese

Tomato, mozzarella and Genovese pesto.

Fresh or Marinated Cabbage

One of the healthiest foods can be finely chopped and seasoned with: salt, olive oil and lemon – vinegar, salt, or light soy sauce and olive oil – alcohol vinegar, salt and left to marinate for a few hours, then squeezed and seasoned with olive and sunflower oil. Eaten immediately or marinated, cabbage keeps for a long time in the refrigerator.

Lemon Marinated Anchovies

Bone the anchovies, salt and sprinkle them with lemon, wait 15 minutes, discard the marinade, repeat the operation until they become white. Wash and dry them very well. Serve them over seasoned radicchio or rocket dressed with lemon juice, olive oil and salt.

Chili powder and chopped garlic are excellent variations.

To make them last a few more days, add a little white wine vinegar to the marinade and keep them in the refrigerator covered with oil in an airtight or vacuum sealed container.

Dutch Salad

Fast and excellent healthy combination: one part of potatoes, two parts of boiled red beets and one part of sliced pickled cucumbers, olive oil, salt and pepper; a little chopped onion is an option.

Lassi

A yogurt drink of Indian origin. The best Lassi is made with canned mangoes that we find in ethnic shops (ripe to perfection). To prepare it, we mix in a blender three parts mango, one part yogurt, one part milk, and one part ice. A delicious healthy drink that is undoubtedly caloric, so we should be careful not to consume too much of it.

Smoothie

We should drink it more often because it is the fastest and easiest way to increase fruit consumption. It doesn't take that long to make, and any fruit will do well. With: just melons or watermelons it is the perfect thirst-quencher – strawberries and a little amount of banana left to macerate with lemon juice and sugar, will satisfy every taste – avocado, milk, and a bit of sugar, is a complete lunch – bananas and kiwi.

All the fruits in season could be mixed with milk or orange, apple, apricot, juices, ice, water; dried fruits and nuts are a nice addition to complement any drink.

Gazpacho

A classic Spanish soup. Easy to prepare, served cold, fabulous in summer, it can be transformed into a super drink. Blend: one part peppers and tomatoes – two parts cucumbers – very little garlic and onion – season with a sprinkle of vinegar and a pinch of salt, and that's it. Chili pepper, ground fennel seeds, and cumin are optional.

Raw Vegetables

Yellow, green and red peppers, cucumbers, fennel, zucchini, and the inner part of celery are used raw, while carrots, pumpkin, green beans, cauliflower must be blanched (boiled a few minutes) – cut into strips or coarsely – seasoned with a sauce made with red wine vinegar and light soy sauce, to our taste. Sesame oil and chili are optional, and excellent results are even achieved with a few vegetables.

The Extractor

Every kitchen should have one since it is one of the most practical way to consume the juices of vegetables, fruits, roots… that maintain their organoleptic, vitamin and enzymatic characteristics. For a good juice, the vegetables must be fresh and pretty cold.

Fennel

Sometimes a vegetable juice can do just good to us.

Let's look at fennel, even if we may not like it very much, we should try it centrifuged (in season everything it is less expensive), it is a refreshing delight, delicious on its own and exceptional with apples added.

Carrots

This beautiful vegetable, with the addition of red beets, is a joy to the palate.

Apples

It is a shame to centrifuge them because blended, cooked or eating the raw avoids any waste, but we will sin because this extract can only make us imagine what the nectar of the Gods is.

Spinach

Instead of eating spinach, we could blend it with a variety of salads and some cucumbers, and if the juice is still a little bitter, adding apples or beets will turn a bland drink into a delight.

Vegetables

Cucumbers, lettuce, peppers, zucchini, and tomatoes in abundance, some celery and carrots, very little onion and garlic, a bit of beet to sweeten, hot pepper, ginger or a few mint leaves, and Parmesan cheese, will make every vegetable concoction very tasty.

Eating less and better means: producing less waste, toxins, and saving energy to the digestive system.

A valid concept for the macrocosm and the microcosm, since minor pollution is in harmony with the planet and our longevity.

Thinking about our health by improving our diet (which is very demanding and difficult to do) puts possession, material things in the background, it becomes a continuous meditation: one of the best forms of inner transformation that helps us live longer and happier.

Homemade Sushi (Sashimi)

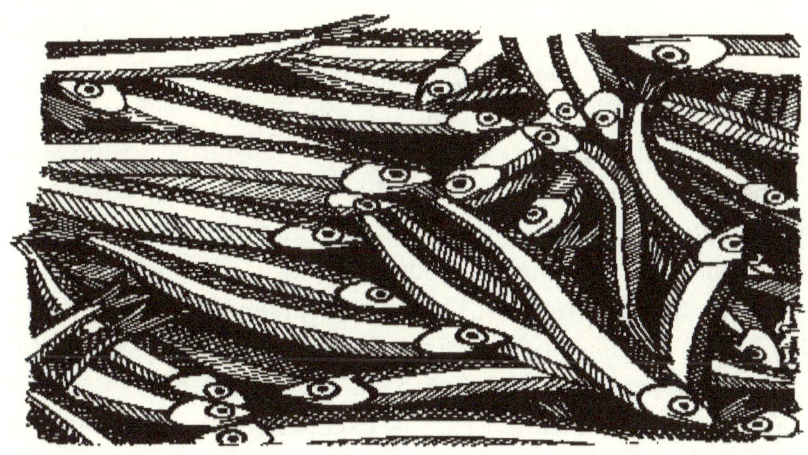

Japanese and especially Chinese people will not be happy with the suggested dish, since it is a home-made copy of a famous dish served in their restaurants. Without special skills required, but really tasty, the proposed version is one of the best ways to increase raw seafood intake. Sea bream, sea bass, perch, salmon, tuna, langostino, anchovies, and some local catch must be freshly frozen and preferably already filleted, while shrimp, squid, cuttlefish and octopus are steamed or boiled.

All seafood cuts should be similar to the classic sushi, and perfection is not necessary as it is for the cut thickness.

We could use Japanese, Basmati, Arborio, Jasmine rice and boil it or use a more professional method that consists of boiling it in a pressure cooker with water (about three times the volume of the rice, it depends on the rice used) to which is added a little salt or light soy sauce, a pinch of sugar, a sprinkle of rice or apple or white wine vinegar, and a little peanut or sunflower oil.

After putting it in the cooker, we wait for it to boil, the lid is then closed and the heat lowered. After about five or six minutes the heat is shot off and the rice is left in the pot for another five, seven minutes (depending on the rice used) to continue cooking.
When ready, it is left to cool off and then transferred to the serving plate. The pieces of seafood are placed on top of the rice seasoned with a mix of light soy sauce and horseradish in the proportions we like. We will use the jar horseradish found in the supermarket (without mayonnaise), and the result will be more than delicious. The quality of our horseradish is usually superior to the Japanese Wasabi imitation found in most supermarkets (based on my experience). Enjoy your meal and remember that the rice is excellent with this sauce, even without fish. We can use salad, arugula, radicchio, and daikon with the rice or instead of the rice.

Boiled Vegetables

They are not bad at all; without potatoes we can eat them at will and lose weight too. They are rich in vitamins, minerals, carbohydrates… Have you ever boiled eggplant or zucchini whole? Cooked whole and then crushed, together or separately, seasoned with olive oil, vinegar, salt or light soy sauce, pepper, a couple of garlic cloves and parsley chopped, it becomes a quick and healthy appetizer. We could make a mix of boiled vegetables with: celery, zucchini, carrots, garlic, onions, cabbage, broccoli, yellow squash, eggplant, cauliflower, pumpkin… And to make any mixing more interesting, we could use various condiments that will also work well with salads, meat and fish:

QUICK AND EASY SAUCES

The ingredients are all minced and blended together, and their order outlines the proportions, which can also vary to our liking.

- Horseradish (in a jar without mayonnaise) and light soy sauce.
- Olive oil, lemon juice or vinegar, salt and pepper.
- Light soy sauce and vinegar.
- Olive oil or sesame oil, vinegar and salt or light soy.
- Parsley, olive oil, vinegar, garlic, chili pepper, salt.
- Oil, mustard, garlic powder, rosemary, vinegar, salt.
- Ketchup and mayonnaise.
- Yogurt, blue cheese, mayonnaise, milk.
- Yogurt, mayonnaise, Parmesan, oregano, garlic, onion powder, pepper.

And finally the wonderful green sauce, special to accompany boiled meats or vegetables.

Italian salsa Verde

For two servings:

A little bunch of blanched parsley, 4 pickled cucumbers, some small pickled onions, 15 capers, 10 anchovies, 3 or 4 garlic cloves, 1 or 2 hard-boiled eggs, pepper to taste, 10 tablespoons of olive oil.

All chopped and blended together.

THREE UNFORGETTABLE HEALTHY SAUCES

Chef's secrets: one of them you certainly do not know, and the other two, since they are secret recipes, are only found on the shelves of some supermarkets.

Nordic

Mustard, chopped pickled gherkins and honey, dill is not-essential, but it is a plus. Special with smoked salmon or boiled meat and fish.

Cocktail

Three, four parts of ketchup (to your taste) and one part of horseradish (common supermarket jar without mayonnaise). With boiled or steamed shrimp over a salad with fresh tomato, it is to die for!

Oriental

One part ginger and five parts carrot. First grated and then blended with a little light soy sauce, to be used as salt, very little sugar and white vinegar, and some sunflower oil.

This beautiful cream of carrots and ginger is the perfect dressing to be used on all crunchy salads: iceberg, romaine lettuce, red radicchio, Belgian endive, and fresh tomato must not be missing.

THE MOST POWERFUL DESCALERS:

GARLIC – LEMON – ONION

Over time, the body accumulates everything: fat, sugar, toxins, etc. Health and longevity depend on the body's ability to eliminate waste and the resulting regenerative power. The best aliments that favor the detoxification process is water, and after it, are garlic, onion and lemon. Eaten raw, they are no longer simple foods, but medicines, they become the most powerful descalers to prevent diseases and premature aging.

Here are some ideas to make their assimilation enjoyable.

GARLIC

A few ways to eat raw garlic.

The best method to eat raw garlic comes from the Argentine and Uruguayan kitchens, where all grilled meat is served with a sauce called:

Chimichurri

A very tasty preparation that also goes very well with grilled or baked fish. The sauce is made of: ½ cup of olive oil, 2 or 3 tablespoons of red wine vinegar, 1 teaspoon of salt, a cup of parsley, 4-5 cloves of garlic and 2 or 3 hot peppers (a depending on their spiciness, and you can also use the dry one), finely chopped. A quick and easy sauce to make that can be embellished with cubes of red, green and yellow peppers.

The sauce is also great without the hot peppers, if we don't like spicy foods.

Tzatziki

A Greek sauce that goes well with grilled meat and fish, can be served as a salad by increasing the dose of cucumbers. It is prepared by mixing together 2-3 grated cucumbers, ½ cup of yogurt, 3 minced garlic cloves and salt to taste. Fresh dill shouldn't be missing, but it is not essential.

Farmer Pesto

Excellent for seasoning pasta and eating lots of raw garlic.

Chop and blend 3, 4 cloves of garlic, a good handful of parsley, some hot red pepper, Parmesan or Pecorino cheese to taste, a few tablespoons of olive oil and a pinch of salt for each serving.

When the pasta is cooked, the sauce is mixed with it.

Other ways to eat raw garlic are with:

Bruschetta: the classic Italian garlic bread served with fresh tomato, garlic and basil – chopped or squeezed in all types of salads, meats, fish – Genovese pesto (with extra garlic) with fresh tomatoes for all pastas – chopped parsley, lemon juice, olive oil, salt, to flavor fish dishes – The bravest will eat garlic with just bread, a pinch of salt and a good olive oil.

Grandfather Marino

A recipe for all remedies: it is not really tasty and shouldn't even be considered a meal. It is a home remedy made with a lot of minced garlic and yogurt.

Garlic is a powerful natural antibacterial and antibiotic difficult to digest raw, and yogurt is fabulous for the digestive system. Therefore, since bigger amounts of raw garlic are easier to ingest and digest with yogurt, together they can strongly counterattack various ailments. To be tried whenever we feel sick (consult your doctor). Finding the remedy to be intense in flavor and difficult to ingest, it can be diluted with milk, water and flavored with rose water and - or cinnamon and honey.

ONIONS

The white ones and the red ones are the most suitable to be eaten raw or marinated. Their powerful purifying properties have been known since ancient times. In the Eastern countries, raw onion is eaten with all types of grilled meat and is never missed with Cevapcici, a famous Balcan dish, and all his other variations.

In India, a popular side dish is onions marinated with lemon, salt and chili. In China, a sauce is made of onions marinated with hot pepper, ginger and salt.

Mexican Chicken Soup

This chicken soup is perhaps the best way to eat raw onion and savor a very simple but delicious traditional Mexican dish. The ingredients for one serving are: half a chicken in pieces without breast, chopped red pepper to taste, a large chopped white onion, about a liter of water, so that at the end of cooking there are about two bowls of excellent broth; and adding lemon juice is traditional but optional. Steps: we boil the chicken for about ten minutes and then add the salt. When cooked: a sprinkle of chopped chili pepper, a squeeze of lemon juice, and only at the end one adds the onion, to keep it fresh and crunchy.

Few calories, healthy, tasty, inexpensive… to try and include in your weekly menu.

Oriental soup

The more liquids we take, the better it is.

Similar to the Mexican soup, because the method and the ingredients are the same, it only varies because the onion is cooked with the chicken and the ginger is minced or sliced (it is fibrous and difficult to digest), and all the ingredients are cooked together. Like the previous soup, it is especially indicated to fight colds; the nose opens on the spot.

Diced celery and chili pepper is suggested.

Here some other easy ways to eat them raw:
With fresh tomatoes seasoned with salt, pepper, vinegar and olive oil or with only ketchup. In all salads. With fresh tomatoes and anchovies. With all smoked fish and grilled meat. Marinated with balsamic or red wine vinegar with olive oil and salt or pickled (the easiest and tastiest way is to use the brine of the purchased pickles (for small amounts). Have you ever tried the classic dish of the old Italian shepherd? Bread with sliced raw white onions, salt and olive oil is a healthy must-try dish that should be eaten more often. You could also try a sandwich called Yin & Yang (my creation) made with raw white onions cut into slices and pitted Taggiasche or Kalamata olives.
It is a very healthy and tasty low-calorie appetite blocker that can be transformed by adding to our taste: salad leaves and sliced tomatoes, peppers and cucumbers.

LEMONS

Lemonades, lemonades, lemonades, whenever it is possible for lunch, dinner, to quench your thirst. Lemon juice with salads, meat, fish… Lemon juice works well everywhere.
A couple of sauces:
Well shaken grated lemon zest and lemon juice, olive oil, a pinch of salt and breadcrumbs – lemon juice, olive oil, salt and black pepper or chili powder and a little water (emulsified), everywhere, – fish broth or beef broth with a little of corn starch or breadcrumbs, ginger or curry (are optional), and lemon juice at the end of cooking. It is a perfect sauce for fish or meat dishes. Lots of lemons to everyone.

AND IT DOES NOT END HERE

Our experience continues and is renewed day by day. I hope you have found this reading enjoyable and interesting.

Now, if my stories and suggestions have rung a bell, it's your turn to start experimenting. This is the purpose of this manual. Start with the most practical exercises and gradually increase your commitment, and your awareness, health, and happiness will benefit from it.

And goooood luck.

Since I consider it extremely useful to share any small or important healing experiences due to: an herb, exercises, a root, a change of thought… I propose to share them on Telegram: "healing expressions" on face-book

With these experiences it's not suggested to do everything on our own, it is always recommended to consult a doctor, but we must not forget that we can do a lot to stimulate healing.

HEALING EXPRESSIONS

Here are some experiences, and the first one is mine.

I cured my throat polyps.

I had sores in my throat, a chronic sore throat, and my throat smelled most likely because I smoked. Therefore, I went for a medical examination and a doctor told me that I had polyps in my throat, and that it was not serious, but that polyps could turn into something else… It has been ascertained that some malignant tumors originate from initially benign polyps.

Alarmed, I took immediate countermeasures: I began to smoke much less, to avoid frozen or very hot drinks and to drink a lot of ginger tea. Noticing that my throat improved, I continued to cure myself mainly with ginger, since I believed that was the key element of the recovery. I went so far as to hold a small slice of ginger in my mouth while I was sleeping, and also to rub my throat with a piece of ginger. I remember I felt like throwing up as I went up and down my throat with that big piece of ginger. Observing also a certain sense of well-being after eating a piece of carrot, I made a carrot and ginger mush in my mouth to compress it against the throat; and I even put myself in the candle position, to more effectively press the mush against the throat. I did many things to heal myself, and after a few months my throat no longer stank, and the polyps disappeared. It is needless to say that we need a specialist to cure us, but since I am convinced that we are capable of hurting ourselves alone, I believe that we can do a lot to help the healing process.

Another interesting case of healing with an alternative medicament is written by Anna, the nephew of Ms. Domenica Del Zotto.

My 90-year-old grandmother was accidentally scratched in the pre-tibial area of her right leg by a dog on May 7, 2012. Resulting in a small wound after the medication in the emergency room, a course of antibiotics was prescribed, and she was then sent to her treating physician, Dr. ‘’ ‘’ ‘’. She visited her and directed her to a district to carry out the periodic medications already prescribed in the hospital emergency room. After about three months of medications (two a week) accompanied by alternating courses of oral and also intramuscular antibiotics, the wound extended more and more to the back of the leg, and the situation worsened to the point that in September my grandmother was sent to the hospital supervised by the Dr. ‘’ ‘’ ‘’ ‘’ ‘’ specialized in ulcers. Having seen the wound, to identify the nature of the lesion, the doctor decided to perform a biopsy. The biopsy was performed on October 2/2012, and the outcome of the histological examination was: “The histological picture, which is not diagnostic, presents some aspects compatible with the clinical picture of a pyoderma gangrenous”.

With this diagnosis, on November 30, 2012, she was sent to the chief physician of dermatology Prof. ‘’ ‘’, who prescribes a therapy with DAPSONE, and since the wound effected deeper tissues and was too extensive, he put her on the waiting list for a skin graft.

Given the continuous expansion and worsening of the wound that also reached the tendon, and considering the explanations I was given about this pathology and the planned treatments to be inconclusive, on December 5, 2012, I decided to start a treatment with honey indicated by Dr. ‘’ ‘’ ‘’ ‘’ (orthopedic surgeon from Cremona).

After three months of bandaging with acacia honey, the area initially affected by the wound (the front part that had received the dog's paw) has completely healed with the formation of a new and resistant skin. After six months the lateral lesion is considerably reduced, and the back lesion, which was the deepest with tendon involvement, reduced in size. Two years after the incident the wound completely healed, and my grandmother is still alive. 03/28/2021.
I will briefly summarize the advantages found with apitherapy:

- effectiveness of the dressing in terms of necessary requirements: controlled humidity, leaving the wound areas dry, avoiding maceration phenomena.
- absorbs excess exudate.
- creates an aseptic environment and prevents the development of infections.
- promotes the spontaneous removal of necrotic parts.
- favors the vascularization which is necessary to start the tissue repair process.
- relieves pain.

To which are added: the relatively simple application does not require special skill or knowledge – the easy availability of raw materials – the very low cost. We only used honey from beekeepers known for the absolute integrity and quality of their products (most of it was honey collected in the Trieste Karst area); we do not know if "industrial-derived" honey can give the same benefit.

The miracle of aloe vera

A few years ago, in my restaurant in New York, a friend of mine showed up all worried because he had a stomach ulcer and the doctor had prescribed him a cortisone treatment that was not working as it should. I remember seeing him swollen in the face and disheartened.

I did not see him then for a while, but the next time he came back to see me, I saw him completely different: he no longer had a swollen face and was really happy because after a long time, he finally felt fine.

I also remember, he told me that he had solved the ulcer problem with the Aloe Vera juice. Treasuring that information, I did some research and discovered that this plant is a real medicine recognized as such all over the world. It is excellent for: the skin, sunburn, (In an emergency, you can't beat the ice. Once, I burned my hand so bad with a firecracker and was in such pain that if I hadn't held in my hand a few ice cubes for hours, I wouldn't have avoided the emergency room) hair, has bacterial properties, and anticancer characteristics are attributed to it. Alexander the Great always had a chariot full of these leaves with him in battles, to heal the wounds of his soldiers... a book on Aloe. Realizing their value and having them available, I started putting the gel all over me, and now I can say that: on the skin, it creates a film that keeps it hydrated – in the *eyes*, with a nice itch (I did it several times, but I let some time pass by, between applications), once I have pulled out a yellow peel, which, even after consulting a doctor, I still don't know what it is – the leaves heal where they are cut (properties that promotes ulcer healing) and in the winter, if kept in a ventilated place in the shade, without any paper or plastic, they keep well up to three months.

Nature Miracles.

Human contact, meeting and discussing face to face, is fundamental: I want to organize a series of meetings to present my book anywhere. To stay updated on where you can find the three essences and the opportunities to meet, follow me on: Facebook: or contact me via email: ilsalutista1@gmail.com

ACKNOWLEDGEMENTS

Thanks to:
my son Nicholas for his general help, my wife Susanna for the patience she had in withstanding everything involved with the creation of this book. They are never appreciated enough.
Justin Perry is the illustrator: jmperry95@yahoo.co.uk
Illustrations, Street art, Murals… he can do it all, a born artist.
Denise Tecchio, the first English corrector, co-director of the American association in Trieste: aia.fvg@gmail.com
Gianpaolo Zecchin "the counselor". The best interior designer in Trieste: documentazioni24@gmail.com
Duilio Cobol "The physiotherapist", the rehabilitation adviser and exceptional massage therapist: d.cobol@libero.it
Georgina Zecchin, an excellent English teacher.gkzecchin@gmail.com
Sharon Edwards, an English teacher friend.
I am in favor of happy endings, I hope that it is everyone's story, and that my experience will help to make everyone feel better and live longer □ □Good luck.

www.ingramcontent.com/pod-product-compliance
Lightning Source LLC
LaVergne TN
LVHW041103150826
845673LV00007B/1902

* 9 7 9 1 2 2 0 0 8 0 5 4 5 *